Women My Husband Married

Other books by the same author:

The Caress and the Hurt

Roses in December

A Backward Look

First printing, November, 1983
Second printing, September, 1985

A Publication Of
GRENFELL READING CENTER
Alamoosook Lake
Orland, Maine 04472

LIBRARY OF CONGRESS CATALOG NUMBER: 83-90468

ISBN: 0-9612766-2-2

PRINTED IN THE UNITED STATES OF AMERICA BY
LITHOGRAPHICS, INC., CANTON, CT 06019

Women My Husband Married

Prose and Verse

Clarine Coffin Grenfell

Clarine Coffin Grenfell

wishing you enduring love

The Reverend Jack Grenfell
1908 – 1980

. . . for Marian Anderson
on the fortieth anniversary of her marriage—
performed with joy, blessed with prayer
by my husband

CONTENTS

DEARLY BELOVED 9

City of Fire
Lightly in Spring
Single
The Auction Wedding

THE HOLY COVENANT 17

Woman
Proposal
Who Giveth This Woman?

FORSAKING ALL OTHERS 37

So Old, So Wise
Something Goes Out of Our Lives
New Voice in Heaven
Mother-in-Love

TO LOVE AND TO CHERISH 53

Condolence Call
Any Fool'd Know Better

WITH THIS RING I THEE WED 63

Lightly in Fall
'Letter of Ordination'
Knowledge
The Little Envelope

WHOM GOD HATH JOINED 79

Somehow I Always Thought
Words, Long After
Deo Volente
The 'Inside' Story

SEND THY BLESSING 115

Christmas, 1943
The Christmas Presents I Remember Best
A Very Special Christmas Present

THE WORLD TO COME 125

Always
Charred Logs
Till Death Do Us Part
'A Sacred Rite'
Prayer of Many Years

TWO MINISTERS TO MARRY was the picture caption when the engagement of the Reverend Clarine Coffin, pastor of the Methodist Church in Dixmont, Maine, to the Reverend Jack Grenfell, pastor of Trinity Methodist Church in Bridgeport, Connecticut, was announced in July, 1937.

. . . DEARLY BELOVED

Dearly beloved, we are gathered together here in the sight of God, and in the presence of these witnesses, to join together this man and this woman in holy matrimony; which is an honorable estate, instituted of God, and signifying unto us the mystical union which exists between Christ and his Church; which holy estate Christ adorned and beautified with his presence in Cana of Galilee. It is therefore not to be entered into unadvisedly, but reverently, discreetly, and in the fear of God. Into this holy estate these two persons come now to be joined. If any man can show just cause why they may not lawfully be joined together, let him now speak, or else hereafter forever hold his peace.

"Let me not to the marriage of true minds
Admit impediments. Love is not love
Which alters when it alteration finds . . . ."

William Shakespeare

THE CITY OF FIRE

And there shall be a City
Where that which we, you and I, have desired
Shall live carnate.

And in this City
There shall be no thing untruthful,
For that is what we, you and I, have desired.
And in this City
There shall be love —
Eros, agape, theos, *all—*
For that is what we, you and I, have desired.
And in this City
The buildings shall be of fire,
The roads of fire,
The air, fire, to cleanse us from our—innocence,
For that is what we, you and I, have desired.

And in this City
There shall be music, but of men, not gods—
There shall be wisdom, but of men, not gods—
There shall be laughter, but of men, not gods—
For that is what we, you and I, have desired.
And in this City
There shall be anger and courage,
There shall be love and courage,
There shall be cleanness of heart, which is courage,
For that is what we, you and I, have desired.

And in this, our fiery City,
There shall be you, there shall be I,
For that is what we, you and I, have desired.

Pamela Margaret Grenfell
Reprinted from ***Current 1965***
Darien, Connecticut

IN THE SPRING

I want to be in love in the spring—
Not a vulgar body passion
That consumes, devours, destroys,
But a tender little love, like a flower . . .

Someone to walk with
Through the hazy twilight . . .
Someone to talk with
Using no words . . .
Someone who'll be quiet
When evening stars are dawning,
Wish on Lady New Moon,
Laugh, and kiss my hair . . .

Someone, will you hurry?
Tulip bugles call you!
Spring is not for laggards—
Someone, come!

SINGLE

I have been lonely for you all my life,
Wanting you, needing you, wishing I were your wife—
Needing your strength when there was much to bear,
Needing your faith when there was much to dare,
Reaching to touch your hand and touching air . . .

I have been lonely for you all my life,
Missing you always, wishing I were your wife—
Longing to share your laughter, grief, or care,
Your joy is all things beautiful and fair,
Turning to see your face and no one there . . .

This word, if no other word I write, is true:
I have been lonely all my life for you . . .
The innermost me that was meant to be your wife
Has been lonely for you, lonely all my life.

THE AUCTION WEDDING
"How Much Am I Bid?"

My husband married a number of interesting women — including me. His marriage to me was the first in which I saw him participate, and he did a creditable job, in spite of the auction.

Four hundred invitations had gone out for the usual rented top-hat, white-satin, four-o'clock affair, but even I was surprised by the size of the crowd milling around outside the church.

"Heavens," I told my oldest brother, "we'll have to pick up more icecream on the way home!" Then through my Juliet veil I dimly saw on the lawn of the house next door a tattered red flag and the bold, black letters of a sign: **AUCTION TODAY 3 P.M.** I thought of Mother's long lists with their dozens of little check marks. She'd followed Emily Post to the letter. Emily should add another letter: Check church neighborhood for auctions.

It was late June, and far too hot to close the church windows on the pew-jammed friends inside. Even with the windows closed, the competition would have been uneven. The auctioneer had an hour's head start and was nearing the peak of his performance. Our man had just come from a funeral and wasn't even warmed up.

Nevertheless, he began bravely, opening his black *Ritual* with slow dignity and speaking in the muted tones befitting a solemn occasion.

"Dearly Beloved, we are gathered together here . . . to join this man and this woman — "

"How much am I bid?" boomed the auctioneer. "Who'll start 'er off?"

The minister gave no sign, but his voice was a little less muted. ". . . which is an honorable estate —"

"Estate of a late millionaire!" cried the auctioneer. "The gen-u-wine article! See here — not a sign o' writin' on 'er bottom!"

I felt the bridegroom stir beside me. Not for nothing had he driven me up and down the hills of Maine to at least a dozen country auctions. He knew as well as I that dishes with no signature are often older and more valuable. But could this 'gen-u-wine article' possibly be the one thing we'd been searching for? Could it possibly be the ironstone soup tureen I needed to complete my grandmother's set?

". . . speak now, or else forever hold his peace!" said the minister with authority.

". . . piece o' gen-u-wine ironstone!" said the auctioneer with even more. Then it was ironstone! It had to be a soup tureen!

". . . for better, for worse — " The minister's voice was considerably louder than when he'd started, but he was not and never would be a match for the auctioneer. Ministers are trained in cloistered seminaries to the sound of murmured prayer. The auctioneer had obviously been born on a midway and barked since birth.

". . . for richer, for —"

"Four I hear! Who'll say five?"

"I will," said the groom firmly. I looked at my Britisher in surprise, but he was only promising to forsake all others and cleave himself unto me forever. I felt the wedding ring slip over my finger. *Must be nearly over,* I thought. *Maybe we can get in on the tail end of the bidding*. But I had forgotten the soprano. She entered the fray with a will, throwing in all two hundred pounds on the side of righteousness and valor.

"Oh, promise me that someday you and I-I-I-"

"High?" sang the auctioneer. "Eight ain't high for an old piece like this. Not a chip! Not a crack! Not a sign o' writin' on 'er! Eight I hear! Who'll say nine?"

It took all my willpower to keep quiet. Naturally I was interested in my own wedding, but ironstone soup tureens are really scarce.

". . . now pronounce that they are man and wife." The minister snapped his little book shut much faster than he'd opened it and gave one last injunction: "Whom God hath joined, let not man —" and for the first time he allowed himself a glance toward the open window, "put asunder."

"Ten-fifty once! Ten-fifty twice! —"

I was soundly kissed there at the altar — a kiss long enough to twitter the unmarried maidens a bit, but not long enough to make the matrons start pleating their handkerchiefs. My husband, as I said before, did a creditable job at the first wedding in which I saw him participate. It was certainly not his fault that above the sacred hush of our nuptial embrace there floated, with an awful note of finality, the triumphant cry of the auctioneer:

"Sold — to the highest bidder!"

Mendelssohn was never marched to any faster. We tore out of that Methodist church faster than John Wesley fled the women of Georgia. The car was waiting on the right, but my wonderful new husband knew the way I wanted to go. He pulled me to the left, fumbling in his swallow-tails for bills. At the auctioneer's table the lady with the 'gen-u-wine article' was pocketing her change.

"Madam," my husband bowed in his best ministerial, British, David-Niven manner, "may I present — my wife? We heard inside the valiant battle you waged, and we congratulate you on your victory, but — " and he waved green bills closer and closer to her suspicious face — "we would so much like this — this lovely old piece, for our new home —"

"Hear! Hear!" shouted the crowd. "Let 'em have it! Let 'em have it!"

"Dear lady, for my bride? As a souvenir of the occasion?"

The dear lady hung onto her prize with both perspiring hands until she had fully comprehended the numbers on the bills. Then she let go the dish, my husband let go the cash, and we ran to the waiting car with the cheers of the crowd in our ears.

"Well," grinned my oldest brother, pushing back his top hat and pushing in the clutch, "guess we finally got the old antique auctioned off. How much did that thing cost you, Rev?"

"Too much," said my husband, "but I couldn't have her go through life wishing she'd gone to the auction instead of the wedding. Besides —" he turned the dish upside down — "I sort of wanted to find out for myself."

"Find out what, dear?" I was foolish enough to ask.

"Why —" he put the dish on the floor and his arms around me — "if there's any sign o' writin' on 'er bottom."

* * * *

It was a huge ironstone platter, not a soup tureen, that the young Reverend and Mrs. Jack Grenfell carried away from the First Methodist Church in Bangor, Maine, that hot June day, and holiday turkeys were served from it for many, many years. For this marriage, perhaps because of its business-like beginning, proved to be a going concern. A few chips, of course. A nick or two here and there. But no cracks. No breaks. The gen-u-wine article in every way.

"Who giveth this woman to be married to this man?" *the Reverend Thomas Grenfell asked at the marriage of Clarine to his son, Jack, June 28, 1938, in the First Methodist Episcopal Church in Bangor, Maine.*

. . . THE HOLY COVENANT

I require and charge you both, as you stand in the presence of God, before whom the secrets of all hearts are disclosed, that, having duly considered the holy covenant you are about to make, you do now declare before this company your pledge of faith, each to the other. Be well assured that if these solemn vows are kept inviolate, as God's Word demands, and if steadfastly you endeavor to do the will of your heavenly Father, God will bless your marriage, will grant you fulfillment in it, and will establish your home in peace.

"Entreat me not to leave thee,
or to return from following after thee:
For whither thou goest, I will go;
And where thou lodgest, I will lodge:
Thy people shall be my people, and thy God, my God:
Where thou diest, will I die, and there will I be buried:
The Lord do so to me, and more also,
If aught but death part thee and me."

from The Book of Ruth, 1:16-17

WOMAN

Adam lies sleeping. God works busily,
Shaping her loveliness, spinning her hair.
Silence in Eden, save the deep murmuring
Bees tell to roses, honeying there . . .
Silence in Eden save when is broken
Sharply the droning by quick slap of clay . . .
Deftly God curves the last sweeping eyelash,
Breathes on it upward, and Woman sees day.

Infinite moments He views His creation,
Startled His image in her eyes to say—
Woman and God, beholding each other.
Comes a low whisper: "Speak Thou to me?"

"Thou art Woman. I, thy Creator,
After long eons of skill and of care,
Make thee—consummate of all earthly beings,
The last and the finest that here I may dare.
Thou art Woman. In earth's great drama
Greatest of all roles I give thee today—
Daughter, wife, sweetheart, sister, mother.
Woman, art able these parts to play?"

"What is a daughter?"

"Dew on white lilacs
Unkissed at dawning by passion of sun—
Laughter, grace, purity, trust, adoration,
To aging lives, immortality won."

"Sister?"

"Is knowing man at his highest,
Banished all subterfuge, jealousy, strife.
Honesty, frankness, tender confiding,
Sweet ministrations, shared throughout life."

"Sweetheart and wife?"

"Is union completed.
One's not enough. Ever restless you'll be
Until in a mate is the earth quest completed,
And two all their seeking turn upward to me."

"Mother?"

"Is sharing my joy in creation,
Splashing a sunset, nurturing a soul,
Curling a white wave, tracing a bluet,
Guarding my stars when the wild comets roll.
Mother is welcoming sacrifice, sorrow.
Love so transforming is hers she can call
Pain, deepest joy and privation, high privilege,
Give all and find thus the meaning of all."

Radiant, glowing, the Woman uprises,
Lifts high her arms to life, pauses to say,
"Tools Thou hast given me, Loving Creator?
Tools Thou hast given, these parts to play?"

"Tool of thy Woman's voice, lovely in laughter,
Cadence of pine trees, laden with tears . . .
Tool of thy healing hands, soothing, caressing,
Comforting heartache, calming all fears . . .
Tool of keen eyes to see suffering, sadness,
Tool of swift sympathy, filling that need . . .
Tool of thy Woman's soul, loving, compassionate,
Transcending evil, Godward to speed."

In quick humility there in the garden
Kneels she before Him and shall kneel alway.
"For the life and the vision, Father, I thank Thee.
For the wisdom, the courage, Father, I pray."

New Milford, Connecticut
1938

PROPOSAL

For the McIntires, with affection . . .

I know a place on top of the world
Encircled by hills and sky,
A place of peace, a place of joy,
Where a flag flies free and high.

In this airy place on top of the world
There is nothing at all to fear—
The petals fall from apple trees,
The little birds sing clear . . .

Come live with me on top of the world
Where rows of spruce trees grow!
Come share red sunsets and pink dawns!
Come walk in the white moon glow!

Come make a home on top of the world
With wide blue sky above,
With good green earth to nurture us—
Come be my own true love!

I'll honor you and husband you
And hold you when you cry . . .
We'll work and play and sing and pray
And love until we die.

Will you come with me to the top of the world?
Will you listen to my plea?
Give me your answer, sweet Charlene—
Will you be wife to me?

Stony Brook Farm
Perham, Maine

WHO GIVETH THIS WOMAN?

"I'm Captain Jinks of the Horse Marines!
I feed my horse on corn and beans,
And I love the ladies in their teens—"

Cloppety, clop, and a clop, clop, clop—the black-tasseled carriage rolled along Mount Hope Avenue, pulled by a bony old white horse who seemed to be keeping time to the carefree singing of a bony old white-haired lady on the front seat. I leaned against the old lady's knee, listening to every word.

"For I'm Captain Jinks of the army!"

"I wish she wouldn't," I heard my mother sputter. "At least not on Sunday." Mama—crowded on the back seat with Merle, Lloyd, Millard Jr., Bart, food for nine living people and flowers for many more dead ones—was trying hard to hang on to her Sunday-go-to-cemetery dignity, but Grammie Pomroy, Papa, Jill, and I on the front seat only wanted to have a good time.

"What are Horse Marines?" I asked. "I thought Marines went in boats."

The old lady cocked her head at me. "Not enough boats," she yelled. "Went clear to Boston in old hay wagons!" She tipped back her head and sang louder than ever.

"When I left home, Mama she cried,
Mama she cried, Mama she cried,
When I left home, Mama she cried,
'You're not cut out for the army!' "

"Everyone's laughing at us," Mama protested again, and almost everyone we passed did seem to be smiling, but at what? My great-grandmother's loud singing? her waving parasol? the purple lilac in Papa's cap? the gangling arms and legs, sticking out from the carriage at all angles, of six assorted children? Or were people perhaps smiling at Mama herself, barricaded as she was behind four boys, three picnic hampers, two stone lemonade jugs, one large urn filled with red geraniums and ivy, and countless mounds of lilacs wrapped in wet newspaper?

"I joined the army when twenty-one.
Of course, I thought it lots of fun,
But from each battle"—

Grammie's voice, overstrained, cracked on the high note, but Papa, Jill, and I, rushing in to help, finished with a bellow loud enough to wake the dead toward whose graves we traveled:

"—I did run,
For I'm not cut out for the army!"

"Millie Coffin, for heaven's sake!" Mama was really exasperated now. "If you have to sing on Sunday, can't you at least sing a hymn? Not that bawdy old music hall nonsense!"

"Grammie can't remember hymns," I called back, "but she saw *Captain Jinks* in New York once. It's the only song she remembers.

"Salute your partners, turn to the right—"

Encouraged by Papa, the old lady shrieked louder than ever, waving the black stick of her parasol from side to side like a baton while Papa, keeping time with the whip, gently tickled old Maud's white rump and Jill and I joined in again—

"And swing your partner with all your might,
And promenade 'round to the right,
For that's the style in the army—"

The tune and the words echoed through my head as I leaned against the black-tasseled carriage on my wedding day. My reception had been at 782 Broadway, the home that Captain Daniel K.

Pomroy's ship's carpenters had built for his bride, my great-grandmother. Today my minister husband and I had stood in the same corner of the parlor where Grammie and her sea captain had greeted friends at their wedding reception, long before the Civil War. I, too, had mingled with guests, tossed my bridal bouquet, and gone up the stairs, supposedly to change into 'going-away' clothes.

Instead, I had crept swiftly down the back stairs, down the steep cellar stairs. Now, holding high the long lace train of my wedding gown, I felt my way over the damp, earthen floor to the black-tasseled carriage and pulled from under its front seat my 'real' going-away bag. Had I been missed? Would my sister Jill become suspicious when I wasn't in the bedroom? Would Rev be able to slip away, too? Would our plan work?

We knew the trouble we'd have if it didn't. I was twenty-seven, Rev thirty. We'd taken part too often ourselves in the wild chasing of the honeymoon car, the blocking of the roads, the teasing all-night phone calls to be let off easily now that our turn had come. Dozens of friends, mostly young married couples, filled the sprawling fifteen-room house, chatted on the lawns outside, compared notes with my Uncle Linwood and my four brothers. All were waiting to have fun with the dignified young British clergyman and his bride.

But Rev and I had made our own plans. All we had to do was get from 782 to the home of Eleanor Rice, two miles away, where our car was hidden. Eleanor, a former student of mine at Bangor High, had earned an A+ in English and was loyal to the death. But how were we to get there? Several friends had promised to drive us, but my brothers had successfully blockaded each car.

The brothers, of course, had each offered, privately and confidentially, to help us get away. Since he was the oldest, Merle assured us, we could certainly trust him. Since he was nearest to me in age, Lloyd confided, and since he and Margaret were hosting our reception, we could surely place our faith in him. Why, he'd even let us have their camp on Long Pond for our honeymoon! Why not?

We both knew why not. My younger brothers, too, had solemnly sworn their loyalty. Millard Jr., however, couldn't keep the grin off his face. Bart, seventeen, had gotten his first driver's license only the day before. He'd done this, he told us, especially to help us get away and had even spent his last cent on an old jalopy for that purpose. Almost I believed Bart, but not quite. A minister friend of Jack's had offered his cottage at Owl's Head, Rockland, for our honeymoon. To each his own. The Reverend Fred Bass was the one we trusted.

Even Uncle Linwood, who'd walked me down the aisle and given me away, had offered to help. With a long face he assured us that he didn't think it was right to give clergymen a hard time on their wedding day. Now he was my father's only living brother, treasurer of the Eastern Trust and Banking Company, and not only that, but a member of the Columbia Street Baptist Church. Surely we could confide in him.

But I had seen too many Maine weddings. I had also seen in the trunk of Uncle Linwood's car several cartons, each filled to the brim with the fine confetti banks produce. Uncle Linwood had obviously been saving waste from canceled checks ever since the year before when I'd put on Rev's diamond.

No, relatives were not to be trusted. Not even my mother, or rather, ***especially*** not my mother. A widow for more than a decade, she had struggled valiantly through depression years to rear and educate six children. Why on earth out of all prospectively well-to-do sons-in-law her older daughter had chosen a penniless Methodist preacher, son and grandson of penniless Methodist preachers, mother could never understand.

Rev, moreover, had made the terrible mistake of sending her a purple bedjacket the previous Christmas. Only old, old women wore purple, and you wore flannel nightgowns to keep warm in Maine. You didn't put on a bedjacket until you went into the hospital to die! What kind of jackass was I engaged to, anyway? She was a long, long way from being dead and would prove it to him.

She did—lived to be ninety-three and for all those years continued to send newspaper clippings of awards and honors won by every lawyer, doctor, engineer, who had ever come out Broadway with even the slightest gleam of love light in his eyes. In the margin of each clipping would be the cryptic message: 'Another one you might have married.'

No, mother, I was certain, would not be at all averse to seeing the four Coffin boys have a real old-fashioned shivaree with a preacher son-in-law. Mother had always been partial to the men of her own family.

And so, I thought, smoothing the velvet seat of the old carriage where my father had so often held me, have I been—partial to the men of the family. *Wish you'd been here today, Papa, to give me away, to answer 'I do.'* Then, as I waited for Rev, I seemed to hear above the music from the rooms upstairs, above the muffled laughter on the lawns a deep voice from far away—

> ***"I'm Captain Jinks of the Horse Marines,***
> ***I feed my horse on corn and beans. . . ."***

The wheels of the old carriage started turning, the back seat overflowed with flowers, and above the smell of the earthen floor I caught a whiff of the cigar smoke I'd smelled many a Sunday afternoon in my childhood, jouncing along in a black-tasseled carriage on the way to a cemetery.

Forebears

Decoration Day was always a happy holiday, the first spring outing after the long Maine winter. Pails of cold water stood on the barn floor at 782 Broadway the day before, and all Saturday six Coffin kids ran in and out, filling the pails with flowers for each one's favorite forebear.

My favorite was Priscilla Pushaw, the Indian princess who'd married my great-great-grandfather, Captain Benjamin Gulliver. Polly, I was quite sure, did not care for cultivated garden flowers. For her I climbed our stone wall, crossed the brook into Hillman's pasture, and braved dozens of black-and-white Holstein bulls on the other side. I never wore anything red on these excursions, for Lloyd had told me these cows were, indeed, all bulls. Merle said not to be a darn fool—how could Charlie Hillman run a milk farm with all bulls? Not quite sure of the difference, I took no chances and wore no red.

Indian moccasins (my mother called them Lady's Slippers) grew on the far slope of Hillman's pasture, along with masses of white and yellow violets and tiny French polygala. I asked Grammie once if Polly was her mother's nickname because she liked polygala, but Grammie said Indians call the flower snakeroot and use it for snake bite. Polly Pushaw, I thought, six feet down in her grave, might very well need a little snake root now and then. For her I braved the bulls. Only once, when at least twenty were lined up along the brook in a particularly ferocious manner, did my courage fail me. I settled that day for the pale green skunk cabbage growing in the marsh on the near side.

My brothers, of course, favored the sea captains. Now and then Merle would tease Grammie by taking a great bunch of Stinking Benjamin for her father's grave, but mostly the boys picked lilacs. Who knew? Perhaps the roots for these lush purple or white trees had been brought from the Orient by the very captains whose graves they now decorated. At any rate, Persian perfume stirred strange longings in New England breasts. My brothers often wished they, too, could sail a clipper ship to China, go around the Horn.

Jill always gathered bluets, tiniest flowers in the world, for the 'Infant' tombstones, and there were many. Tenderly my younger sister would lay her wilted offerings before the small marble markers of children who had died before they were even named—'Infant Son of—' or 'Infant Daughter of—'

Jill's favorite child had a name we all knew, though, and she had heard Grammie Pomroy tell his story so often that she knew it by heart.

"He died of diphtheria!" Kneeling before the curved marker of Millard Fillmore Pomroy, son of Captain Daniel K. Pomroy and his wife, Margaret, Jill would recite the story mournfully. "He begged for a drink, but the doctor said ***'No!'*** He was burning up with fever, but the doctor said ***'No!' 'Wawa, Mama,'*** little Millie begged, but the doctor said ***'No!'*** and so he died, and he was only four years old—"

"And everyone said," Grammie took up the tale of her only son, "he was too beautiful to put into the ground. Long, auburn curls, he had, and red cheeks—and now the doctors say ***'Give water! Give all the water they can drink!'*** and he died, begging me for water—begging me—" And even after seventy years the old lady's voice would be heavy with grief as she told of the thirst of her dying child and her misplaced trust in the doctors of long ago.

So Jill gathered her small blossoms for the Infants, the boys used the iron rake to pull down the top branches of the lilac trees, and I came home from Hillman's pasture with wet feet and baskets of violets and snake root. By dusk on the eve of Decoration Day every pail would be overflowing so that even old Maude in her stall below the barn floor must have had a fragrant night's sleep. She needed it. Decoration Day was always a strenuous affair.

Six days a week my father would leave early in the morning for and come home late at night from his job as cashier for the American Railway Express Company, but on the seventh day he belonged to us. We buzzed around him, eager to please—polished the black carriage till we could see ourselves in its sides, dusted the velvet seats with the whisk broom, straightened the tangled tassels around the top, filled the deep lamp wells with kerosene. Mount Hope was seven miles from 782. It might well be dark before Old Maude got us home. Really a farm horse, on week days Maude pulled a harrow or a hay rake as we cultivated our eight acres, but on Sundays she became a carriage horse, scrubbed and curried to a milky whiteness.

Mother packed the picnic baskets—cold roast chicken, homemade bread and butter, dozens of apple turnovers, soft molasses cookies, lemonade. Jill and I, called to squeeze the lemons, squeezed with all our might, but Mama could always come along and press out a few more drops. Then we'd be sent to take the flowers from the pails, wrap them in wet newspapers, stuff them between the stone jugs so none would crack. When all was ready, Papa helped Grammie Pomroy carefully down the steep curved stairwell she'd skipped over so heedlessly as a sixteen-year-old bride and lead her, leaning heavily on her parasol, round to Old Maude.

"Here's your bit of sugar," she'd say. "You've got a hard day's work ahead of you, Maude," and then, to my father, "Heist me up, Millie." Up she'd go, onto the front seat between me and Jill, with Papa on the far side, Mama and the boys in back. Old Maude would turn her head and sadly survey the nine of us. "I know who you are," she seemed to say, "and how many there are of you, and where we're headed, and what a long hard haul it is."

"Never mind, old girl!" Papa gave her a cluck. "The boys and I'll walk the hills, and there's no rush. Everybody there'll wait for us."

Papa and the boys did jump from the carriage and walk the hills, Grammie kept us lively with ***Captain Jinks,*** and in an hour or so we were climbing the steep, rutted slope to the oldest part of the ancient burying ground.

Mount Hope is no ordinary flat graveyard. Re-designed in the 1830s by the architect Charles Bryant, it is considered the first 'garden cemetery' in America. Stretching up from either side of a broad

THIS INDIAN CHIEF was always in Margaret Pushaw Gulliver Pomroy's home. Is it a bust of her grandfather, Chief Pushaw?

THE BLUE LADY, oil on canvas, was brought from Scotland by Captain Benjamin Gulliver in 1780.

brook, it follows the natural contours of hill and valley, and from each hill one can see the mighty Penobscot, rushing past on the other side of the main road.

Papa unharnessed Old Maude, the boys brought water from the brook for her and for the tin vases we stuck deep into the earth. Grammie sorted the flowers, making sure no mound of ours, no matter how renegade its occupant, went undecorated. Then Mama, busy with hampers, gave the welcome call, "Come, now!" Sprawling on the fine soft grass, the nine of us circled the picnic cloth. This was the best time, the time for food and family legend.

"What's your name, dearie?" Merle asked the question that never failed to start Grammie off.

"My name," the stately old lady answered with all the dignity of her ninety-plus years, "is Margaret P. Peggy Pushaw Gulliver Pomroy Coffin."

"Not Coffin," Lloyd contradicted. "You're not really a Coffin, Gram. Your daughter married a Coffin. You're a Margaret P. Peggy Pushaw—"

"Tell us about her!" I'd interrupt. "Tell us about Polly Pushaw and the scalping—" Millard Jr., Bart, and Jill would all be clamoring with me, and the old lady, sure of her audience, was eager to oblige.

"That's her stone," she'd say, pointing. Her name was Priscilla, but everybody called her Polly. And that's her husband's—Cap'n Ben Gulliver. Sailed his ship from Scotland up the Penobscot to Bangor just after the Revolution. Liked the river town so well he decided to settle here and built his house way out on Broadway. It's still there—you all know, where your Aunt Fannie lives. Cap'n Ben did a lot of trading with the Penobscot Indians, who were all around and friendly, but one winter there was a famine. Even the Indians were short of food, and when they knocked on my father's door and asked for food, he refused. The next day—"

"He was out in the woods," Lloyd interrupted, "tryin' to shoot a squirrel or somethin' to eat when he felt a knife at his back. 'Food,' said the Indian. 'Food or scalp.' "

" 'Food it'll be,' " Gram, who didn't like her stories taken away from her, went on. " 'Just let me go home and I'll give you all I've got.' The Indian kept his knife point at the Cap'n's back all the way home. The Cap'n gave him his last sack of dried beans and all the salt pork he had. The Indians were grateful. That spring Chief Pushaw himself appeared at the Cap'n's door with a thank-you present—his daughter Priscilla, a beautiful, black-haired, black-eyed Indian princess.

" 'She's yours,' said the Chief, 'for pork and beans.' The Cap'n took one look at Priscilla and decided this was the best trade of his life. So they were married and had fifteen children in that house, and here they lie side by side—the Indian and the Scotsman, my mother and father. . . ." And Grammie reached out her quivering old hand with the raised blue veins and traced the two names on the marble stones.

"Was she really a princess?" Merle asked skeptically. "And if she was, why did she have to beg for food?"

"Every Indian girl who married a white man was a princess," Papa laughed, "but maybe she was one at that, for Pushaw Pond is named for her family."

"Pond!" Grammie sniffed. "Any place 'cept Maine 'twould be called Pushaw Lake, or even Pushaw Sea, for it's fourteen miles long, and my mother's family knew every inch of it from Oldtown to Bangor and beyond, and sped over it in their canoes, for the Penobscots could make faster canoes than any other tribe, 'n I hear now they're shipping them all over the world—"

"Canoes!" Papa would say scornfully. "What good's a canoe if you want to go whaling? The Coffins were whalers, Gram—the Coffins your daughter married into. Why, they wouldn't set foot in a little puddle like Pushaw Pond! Sailed all over the world, they did, from New Guinea to Newfoundland and back again, in ships, Gram—not birchbark!"

"Huh!" Grammie would toss her head. "You don't have to be a whaler to sail all over the world, Millie Coffin. I've been there, and so has your mother. Sat for our portraits in Antwerp, bought our furnishings in Paris, and as for that tribe of Quakers on Nantucket Island, why, it took them two hundred years to get as far as the Penobscot! Squatted down on the first land they came to and just sat—"

"Didn't do much sitting," Papa disputed.

"Tell us," we'd cry. "Tell us about old Tristram and the whales!"

"Well, things were mighty rough in England in 1642—" Papa'd take up the tale of his side of the family. "Cromwell had driven Charlie out of London—a nincompoop king, if there ever was one—and there was talk of cutting off his head.

" 'Let's pack up and sail for America,' Tristram said to his wife. 'Devon, that used to be a peaceful shire, is now no more than the

Devil's doorstep, with Roundhead and Royalist killing each other, and every man at odds with his neighbor.'

"So sail they did, on the good ship ***Hector***—Tristram and Dionis, their five children, his mother, and two old maid sisters. Landed north o' Boston and stayed there awhile, but there were too many do's and don't's on the mainland even then to please Tristram, so, when he heard he could buy some off-shore islands for only thirty pounds—"

"And two beaver hats," Millard Jr. added.

"Right, son. Mustn't forget the beaver hats. Guess they were sorry come winter, a hundred miles out in the Atlantic. Moved the whole family to Nantucket, and there they stayed, most of 'em, for the next couple centuries and some of 'em are still there, on the beautiful island—"

"Beautiful, my foot!" Grammie snapped. "Have you ever been there, Millie? Well, I have—sand and crabgrass and stinking whale oil! Barely a tree on the whole place—"

"Was that where you heard the death carts, Grammie?" Jill asked anxiously. "Was it that island?"

"Land sakes no, child. That was off the West Indies, a thousand miles south! Dying like flies, the people were, from the yellow fever. Too many for the living to dig a decent grave for. Night after night we lay in the harbor, listening to the death carts rumble through the streets, picking up the dead and carrying them to a common grave. Then we'd see the flames shoot up and smell the awful stench of burning flesh, and the ***Hosea Rich*** in quarantine, for they thought the ships brought the fever—"

"How long did they keep you there? A year?"

"Seemed like a year, Merlie, but 'twas only a month—long enough, with Eva and Lillie racing all over the ship and driving Cap'n Daniel almost crazy—"

"Was it there Eva fell through the hatch with her teddybear?" Papa asked, knowing it was, but wanting to hear again the story of his own mother.

"You know it was, Millie Coffin—and a blessed miracle she had the big teddybear in her hand to catch on the cross bar, and a blessed sailor that flung down a rope and skun after her, else you'd not be here today, Millie Coffin—you and your whales—no, and not one of you young ones either." And Grammie would glare at us savagely, as though we were the careless ones who'd left the hatch open, and all six Coffins would snuggle deeper into the sun-soaked grass of the cemetery, glad to be alive and shivering to think how, save for one big teddybear, one brave sailor, and one wooden crossbar, they might never have been—no, not one of them. . . .

"A BLESSED MIRACLE she had the big teddy bear in her hand to catch on the crossbar, or you'd not be here . . . no, not one of you!"

'A Man Who Would Love the Sea . . .'

So the Decoration Days had worn on, and the years had worn on as, all through my childhood, I listened to tales of the men of my family and dreamed of a man as brave as they, a man who would love the sea. I wrote verses about this, and Grammie liked to listen to them. Perhaps because she'd been fathered by a sea captain and married to a sea captain, she especially liked one I wrote during my first year in college:

And will I marry you, my love,
And will I e'er be true?
I cannot tell, my love, until
I see the sea with you . . .

Until I lie beside your side
To watch the white gulls write
Their lovely curving messages
Across the sky in white . . .

For Viking blood is in my veins,
In my heart wanderlust!
Since I shall love the sea alway,
*The man I marry must!**

"Stick to that," Grammie'd said, "and you'll not go wrong."

Soon after that, we had ridden to Mount Hope Cemetery for the last time with Margaret P. Peggy Pushaw Gulliver Pomroy. The ride had seemed very quiet that day, with no one singing, and under my breath I had said the words:

"When I left home, Mama she cried,
Mama she cried, Mama she cried.
When I left home, Mama she cried,
'He's not cut out for the army!' "

I had 'stuck to that,' and I hadn't 'gone wrong,' I thought, picturing with joy the tall, handsome Cornishman who had stood beside me that day at the altar. I'd had to wait longer than some, but I hadn't gone wrong. Strange and wonderful are the ways of love,

**SONG OF THE VIKING'S DAUGHTER*
From ***The Caress and the Hurt***

and strange and wonderful it seemed to me that, nearly three hundred years after old Tristram had sailed from Plymouth Harbor for the New World, another ship had sailed from that same Harbor, bearing a boy with a burning love for the sea in his heart. Born in Land's End on the very tip of Cornwall, playing his boyish games in Penzance caves the pirates knew, growing up with the roar of the wild Atlantic surf always in his ears—Jack Grenfell had come to America and found Clarine Coffin as naturally as though their families had left Plymouth on the same ship, the same day, and not three hundred years apart.

THE ROAR OF SURF was always in their ears as Jack, Dick, and Tom Grenfell, Jr., were growing up in St. Ives.

"Who giveth this woman to be married to this man?" the minister had asked, there at the altar, and Uncle Linwood, speaking for all the men of my family, had answered, ***"I do."*** Now in the stillness of the old cellar of Captain Daniel's home, there came a sort of whispering, a faint, friendly rustling—as though Captain Daniel himself and Captain Benjamin and Tristram in his whaleboat and Chief Pushaw in his fleet canoe, and my father, who had taught me to love the sea, were all there around the black-tasseled carriage, all nodding their heads in happy agreement, all saying, "Aye, aye, sir. We do. We give her to you. We, too . . ."

There were steps on the cellar stairs. My husband came forward out of the shadows and took my hand.

"It's no good, dear. The boys have blocked us in completely—there's no way out."

"There has to be!" I opened the outside door a crack. Bart's old jalopy, two cars ahead of it, was parked on the edge of Mrs. Allen's lawn and peony bed next door. Maybe—just maybe. After all, I was ten years older than Bart. He was used to taking orders from me. He'd been doing it all his life.

"Come on! We'll make a run for Bart's car."

"But he'll just call the others—and he's blocked in!"

"Come on!" Rev grabbed my bag and we ran for the car, lay down, white satin and all, flat on the floor of the back seat.

"Mmm—this is nice. Maybe we could honeymoon right—"

Someone was coming, whistling. Bart opened the car door, glanced back, turned as white as my gown. I raised my head, looked my youngest brother straight in the eye, spoke in my most authoritative, school-teacher voice.

"Get in, Bart, and drive like the devil." He hesitated only a second, loyalties divided—adored older brothers, adored older sister. Then he jumped in, started the motor with a roar, drove around the two cars in front of him, straight across Mrs. Allen's lawn and peony bed, down Broadway. No one paid any attention. It was only Bart, showing off his jalopy. We were a mile down Broadway before he could speak.

"Thought you were dead," he said, glancing back. "Scared hell out of me. Where are we going? Uncle Linwood called twenty-eight garages, trying to find your car."

I told him. We were there almost before I got the words out of my mouth.

"Now what?"

"Go back. Help them hunt for us. Pretend this never happened."

He did. An hour or so later when we called from Rockland they were still searching the fifteen rooms, the cellar, attic, sheds, barn. Mother was angry, of course.

"You might have stayed around—let the boys have a little fun. How in the world did you get away?"

They found out, of course. Bart was banned from the family. When Rev and I arrived at our Connecticut parsonage after our brief honeymoon on Owl's Head, we found Bart sitting on the front doorstep. He enrolled in New Milford High, stayed for six months.

And the sea captains who'd whispered ***"We do"***? I told Rev about them. He didn't laugh.

"We say the Creed every Sunday, darlin'—***'I believe in the communion of saints.'*** Where else would sociable, sea-going old saints be more likely to commune than at a sea-loving daughter's wedding party?"

THE FIVE POINTS AT ST. IVES, CLODGY, on the north coast of Cornwall, noted for their raging seas, fierce storms . . . "Are the boats all in? Are the men safe," Jack, growing up here, would often waken his parents in the night to ask.

. . . FORSAKING ALL OTHERS

Wilt thou have this man to be they wedded husband, to live together in the holy estate of matrimony? Wilt thou love him, comfort him, honor and keep him, in sickness and in health; and forsaking all other keep thee only unto him so long as ye both shall live?

"There is no more lovely, friendly, and charming relationship, communion, or company than a good marriage."

Martin Luther

SO OLD, SO WISE . . .

The children sit at small tables
On the first day of Sunday School,
Look up at the old one,
The wise one,
The teacher . . .

If you are so wise, they ask,
Why do planes carry death in the skies?
Why do children starve?
Why is my brother a pothead?

If you are so wise,
Why are there wars and killing
And yellow smog over cities
And why is my sister a floozie?

If you are so wise,
Why is my mother a drunk?
Why does my father beat me?

The children sit at small tables
On the first day of Sunday School,
Look up at the teacher and ask
"What do you have to teach us?
You who are so old, so wise?"

SOMETHING WARM AND TENDER AND GOOD

Something goes out of our lives when old ones die—
The old, old ones who were old when we were young . . .
Those who held out their hands as we learned to walk, their steps
Unsure, uncertain, too, picked us up when we fell,
Laughed aloud when at last we stood . . . something goes out . . .

Something goes out of our lives when old ones die . . .
The ones who walked tremblingly, yet took us each day
To the park, to the zoo, taught us to look both ways
When crossing streets, stood a long, long while before
The tiger's cage, let us feel the elephant's ear,
Hear monkeys chatter . . . something goes out of our lives . . .

Something goes out of our lives when cold earth falls
On blue-veined hands that held old story books,
Turned pages slowly, gave plenty of time to look
At favorite pictures . . . something goes out of our lives . . .

Something goes out of our lives when tall ones fall—
Those who tossed us, caught us, boosted us high to sit
Behind the wheel in the fire engine down the street,
Fumbled but always found as we walked home
Thin dimes for ice cream cones . . . something goes out . . .

Something goes out of our lives when old ones die—
The old, old ones who were old when we were young . . .
Something warm and tender and good goes out of our lives . . . .

NEW VOICE

For Ethel Rowe Grenfell, 1874-1951

There's a new voice in heaven! O God, can you hear
My own precious Grandma, so good and so dear,
Singing the carols, loud and clear?
She's joining right in with the angels, I know,
Praising the Savior she served here below,
The Jesus she taught me to love and to know.
Our house here seems empty and quiet-like, too—
No Grandma to call as I go racing through.
***"Come, Pammie!"** she'd say, and I miss her, I do.*
So, God, if you've some little angel up there
Whose halo needs straight'ning, whose wing has a tear,
Please give her to Grandma this Christmas so she
Won't be lonesome and missing her own child—that's me.

Bayside, New York
1951

MOTHER-IN-LOVE

"I love"—are the first two words Jack's mother ever said to me. The last two were written in a letter sent to me at Methodist Hospital in Brooklyn, New York, where I was a surgical patient. She and my sister Jill were caring for the children—John, nine, Lorna, seven, Pamela, two.

"How very thankful we are," she wrote, ***"that the trouble is removed! I have prayed constantly for you, dear. You know there is no Friend like our Heavenly Father, who is present at all times in joy or pain . . . Jill has taken hold wonderfully. The children seem to love her, and I think even Pam realizes the relationship. But I know how you must long to see them. Cheer up and come home smiling as soon as it is safe to do so. Your loving Mother G—"***

Fifteen years lay between that first ***"I love—"*** and that last *". . . loving Mother"*—fifteen years of nothing but love, for Ethel Rowe Grenfell, my mother-in-law, was truly my mother-in-love.

"You married me," Jack Grenfell would often say, "because you fell in love with my parents." Perhaps he was right. He'd been proposing marriage, half jokingly, half seriously, for several months before I first walked up the steps of his parents' parsonage in Easton, Connecticut. His mother stood in the doorway, her arms open wide. ***"I love,"*** she greeted me in that deep, warm Cornish voice, ***"the girls that love my boys!"***

I looked at her in surprise. Did I love her 'boy'? He was no 'boy'—twenty-eight to my twenty-five. We'd each been dating for nine or ten years before we'd met each other the previous fall at

Hartford Theological Seminary, and I, at least, had gone on dating others until well after Christmas. Jack had been too busy with his student parish in nearby Bridgeport, sixty miles from campus, to do much dating. Furthermore, one doesn't 'love' quite so easily at our ages. If I 'loved' this handsome, black-haired Cornishman, I certainly hadn't admitted it—to him or to myself. His parents had moved to Easton only the week before. I was in their home not as their son's fiancee, but simply as guest preacher in his church the next morning. What in the world had he been telling his mother?

We went into the parsonage. The Reverend Thomas stood up from behind the tea table and greeted me somewhat formally. We'd arrived an hour later than expected. Tom liked his four o'clock tea at four o'clock. We sat down to it at five—cucumber sandwiches, watercress from a neighbor's brook, saffron bread, cheese, and a large jar of small, white pickled onions.

At nine o'clock we had the same tea all over again—cucumbers, watercress, saffron bread, cheese, and many more pickled onions. Only apples and a small pound cake had been added.

"Don't they ever eat a meal?" I whispered to Jack as the tea things were being cleared away. I didn't care much for pickled onions. I always get hungry when I'm nervous. As Sunday morning's sermon got closer and closer, I was getting hungrier and hungrier.

"Cooked meal every day, dear—at noon. Sorry. We missed it." He slipped another apple into my pocket.

Ethel and Tom talked for a bit—asked about my family in Maine, my teaching, and did I really want to be a woman minister? How many women were there in the Seminary?

Only two, I told them, and perhaps I wouldn't preach. I'd had a course in college I liked—literature of the Bible—taught by the Dean. Maybe I'd teach a course like that. After awhile they said goodnight, hoped I'd sleep well, went upstairs.

Jack, leafing through his black ***Ritual,*** handed it to me open to the ***Order for the Administration of the Sacrament of Baptism.*** A baby was being baptized next day. Would I share the sacrament with him?

I read the paragraph he pointed to—"***. . . that this child, surrounded by steadfast love, may be established in the faith . . . confirmed and strengthened in the way that leads to life eternal.***"

"Well—I'll take it upstairs, look it over . . . need to go over my sermon, too."

"Don't want to come for a walk? It's starlight . . . goodnight then, darling. Don't worry about your sermon. You'll do just fine."

I was halfway up the stairs when I heard my name—"Clarine . . ."

"Yes?" I turned back, but no one was there. Again I started up the stairs.

"Clarine . . ." A man's voice. What was this? I stopped in the upstairs hall, looked around. One door was partially open. Two white-haired people in long white night clothes were kneeling by the bed—hands folded, eyes closed, faces uplifted.

". . . strengthen her spirit, dear God, give her courage to share her deepest convictions and her faith . . . In Jesus' Name. Amen." Then the woman—"Our Heavenly Father, we thank Thee especially tonight for this beautiful girl our son has brought into our home. Be with her tomorrow as she leads his people in worship. We ask Thy special blessing on Clarine . . ."

I went into the guest room, closed the door quietly, leaned against it. They were praying for me . . . for me. Never before had I heard anyone lift up my name to Almighty God . . . and so confidently, so assuredly, as though there were no doubt at all that God was listening, would hear, would honor . . . "We ask Thy special blessing on Clarine . . ."

I looked down at the small black book in my hands, brushed tears from the page, read again the words: ***". . . surrounded by steadfast love, may be established in the faith . . ."*** Perhaps, just perhaps, this Grenfell family was one where I, too, might be ***"surrounded by steadfast love, established in the faith . . . confirmed and strengthened in the way that leads to life eternal."***

The next afternoon when Jack Grenfell—on his knees gathering more watercress for tea from the neighbor's brook—looked up at me and said, "You were wonderful this morning, dear, so natural with the baby . . . by the way, will you marry me?" he nearly fell into the brook when I answered.

"June's a nice month for weddings. Today's the 28th. How about two years from today? We'll both have our degrees—"

Two years later on May 28th we were granted our Bachelor of Divinity degrees. The Seminary gave me the $50 prize for 'excellence in Greek'—enough to buy a wedding dress—and the New York East Conference gave Jack a full-time church. So on June 28, 1938, I wore the wedding dress in Bangor, Maine, and we moved into the parsonage beside the full-time church in New Milford, Connecticut.

The decision made as I brushed tears from Jack's ***Ritual*** surprised him, surprised me, but obviously did not surprise his mother. It was a decision I never regretted. God moves in mysterious ways to bring joy to His children. Was it by chance that I did not walk under the stars that night? that I came up the stairs at that particular moment? that a door into the room of two very private people was not fully closed?

"Heavenly Father," I had heard them pray, "we ask Thy blessing on Clarine—" God did bless my life, and His blessing came through them. So long as they each lived, they were His instruments.

Ethel Rowe Grenfell was a large-boned, broad-shouldered, funny, rollicking woman with snapping dark eyes, dark skin, and white hair that had once been black. "Call me 'Mother G,' if you like," she said soon after our marriage, but the G soon dropped off and she became simply 'Mother.' Years later when I visited Cornwall, I saw many women who reminded me of Mother — who walked, talked, and sang as she had done. Warm and vibrant when she spoke, a deep, pulsing contralto when she sang, her voice was her most notable feature. People often refer to the beauty of Welsh voices, but Cornish singing seems to me more moving, more poignant.

In August, 1972, Jack was invited to preach the 100th anniversary sermon at Bedford Road Methodist Church in St. Ives — the lovely pink granite building designed by his grandfather, John Grenfell, and Tom's first parish church. Three hundred people filled the sanctuary that day, but the organist led them as he might have done a single choir. Some hymns had eight or nine verses. None were omitted. Voices sank low, almost to a whisper, then rose again — ardent, triumphant — swelled to full, soul-stirring volume. Fred Webber, son of Tom's sister Grace, leaned over, steadied my arm, for I could not sing that morning for weeping. All around me were remembered tones of Mother's voice.

She was in her sixties when I met her, had been a minister's wife for thirty-five years, and loved being one, loved the church—***"We love the place, O God, wherein Thine honour dwells."*** Her mother, she told me laughingly, often scolded her for attending too many services. "Hetty would leave the sheets on the line and the beds unmade, and go off to Chapel." When other Grenfell cousins, Bernard and Vera Cogan, took us to the Wesleyan Chapel in St. Just to which 'Hetty' had 'gone off' so frequently, we could understand its appeal for her.

JOHN GRENFELL in his pony cart by Bedford Road Methodist Church in St. Ives, Cornwall in 1872.

Built to seat 1800 people—though often, the records say, 'more than 2000 crowded into this grand building'—it is Methodism's largest, most towering edifice in all Cornwall. John Wesley, who preached in St. Just twenty-eight times over a span of nearly fifty years, often comments in his ***Diaries*** on the fervor and piety of its people. There were worship services, prayer meetings, or class meetings every night of every week when Ethel was growing up, and she herself was one of thirty-eight class leaders.

People who sailed for America from Plymouth Harbor often wrote back that their last glimpse of Cornwall had been the tall spire of the Wesleyan Chapel at St. Just. So it must have been for the Grenfells, and how small, plain, and bare of beauty those Methodist buildings in Connecticut, Kentucky, and Ohio must have seemed to Ethel and Tom after the magnificence and elegance of St. Just, of Bedford Road!

Ethel tried always to make her parsonages more beautiful. Often homesick in those early years, she once confided, she must, I think, have missed not only the beauty of Cornish chapels, but even more the loveliness of Cornish gardens. Wherever she lived, she gardened. Early each morning, late each evening she would be out digging, weeding, cultivating. And always she planted roses.

"Would you like to help me water the garden?" she asked between five o'clock and nine o'clock teas on that first visit. She had moved to Easton from New York City only a week before—unpacked cartons were scattered all about—but June was late for roses. Already Ethel had been to the nursery, bought and planted two Dorothy Parker climbers, for she always chose this rose. Landscaping was not in Methodist budgets in those days, and an itinerant ministry, moving every two or three years, had neither energy nor money for perennials. But wherever she went, Ethel planted her Dorothy Parkers—and when she moved, she left them behind.

"That minister's wife must be like Grandma," Lorna exclaimed happily as we once pulled up in front of a new parsonage. "See? She planted roses!" True enough. There by the back door in full bloom was a beautiful bush of yellow roses. We watered faithfully, enjoyed it fully for a week. Then one evening as Pamela stood, hose in hand, a car pulled into our drive.

"We've come for our rose bush," the wife of the previous minister wasted no time on amenities. "It's ours. We bought and paid for it." Her husband took spade and burlap from their trunk. The children watched silently as the rose bush was dug up, put into the trunk, carried off—yellow petals falling all along the drive.

"That woman," John summarized the situation in his usual succinct way, "isn't at all like Grandma." The children never called her by name. Always she was simply 'the woman who came and dug up the yellow rose bush.'

One cannot write about Ethel without writing about Tom, for her life revolved around him. He was her opposite in many ways. Courtly, dignified, dressed always in clergy clothes — Tom was never seen without his stiff, white clerical collar, black vest, pince-nez on a black ribbon. In summer he changed from black Homburg to white Panama, from black wool to white flannel. Otherwise his ecclesiastical garb stayed the same. Fair-skinned, pink-cheeked, white-haired, his most striking feature was his luminous, unusually large blue eyes. Only our daughter Lorna is fortunate enough to have inherited Tom's eyes.

I like to think of him the day the Grenfells left Cornwall. The day was July 4, and so the American captain called everyone on deck for a brief observance of the holiday. The Reverend Grenfell, the captain said, was on his way to an American church and would lead in prayer for his new country. Then all on board would join in singing ***The Star-Spangled Banner.***

Tom led in prayer, but all did not join in singing ***The Star-Spangled Banner***. Most, in fact, dropped out '***. . . at the twilight's last gleaming.***' All but the five Grenfells. They might have grown up singing ***God Save Our Gracious Queen***, they might still be able to glimpse, back there over the waves, the tall spire of St. Just Chapel, but they were on their way to America, and Tom had made sure they were ready—ready for a new country, a new home, new schools. All four verses of ***The Star-Spangled Banner*** had been thoroughly memorized. Now, in strong, vibrant Cornish voices, all four verses were sung.

"You never heard such a cheer as went up," Mother, always astonished that only Grenfells had known the words, would end the story. But Grenfells looked ahead, not back. Tom never joined a St. George Society, never romanticized 'Old England.' They were in America now. They would be Americans.

Tom's second impressive characteristic was his marvelous command of language. His vocabulary, fluency, and faultless use of words never failed to thrill and amaze this former English teacher.

He came to live with us in Bethel the winter after his leg amputation. John was two months old. All during those long months of recuperation, Tom sat by the fireplace, grandson on his one good knee, talking, talking, talking to the wide-eyed baby, reading aloud the ***Psalms***, the ***Epistles***, quoting Scripture, Shakespeare, saying prayers.

It was a difficult time for the courtly British clergyman, waiting for the stump to heal so that a steel leg might be attached. We turned our faces away as Tom crawled on hands and knees up and down the long stairway. Yet ***"All things,"*** the Apostle tells us, ***"work together for good to those that love the Lord."*** Tom's grandson, too, has a marvelous vocabulary, a remarkable fluency of language. Sometimes, listening to John preach, I hear a turn of phrase, an intonation, that take me back thirty years to another pew, another sermon, another voice.

Tom was also a tease. "You're the cream in my Coffin," he'd said without a trace of smile, passing the cream pitcher to Jack at that first five o'clock tea. And he was generous. "Can't think what to give you," he wrote to me one Christmas. "Come down and we'll go shopping."

He took me to Read's in Bridgeport, led me to the expensive dress department, pointed to a rack of velvet gowns. "Why not try on that blue one—color of your eyes." It was the kind of extravagant, foolish thing my own remembered father might have done. I wore the blue velvet with pride—and gratitude—for many Christmases. Ten years later Ethel made it over for Lorna, five years after that for Pamela. Finally it became a doll's dress—still in a trunk somewhere.

"What are you doing, dear?" Tom stood by my desk. "You've been there an hour with your face screwed up."

Trying to figure out a bill, I told him. How much did the Woman's Society of Christian Service owe me? I was secretary of spiritual life for the district, had traveled to several meetings. Officers were paid five cents a mile. Did they owe me $3.85 or $4.60? How far was it to New Haven, anyway?

Dad took out his wallet, laid a five-dollar bill on the desk. "Tear it up, dear. Don't ever be afraid to be generous with God."

Tom and Ethel were not afraid. They tithed their small salary, yet somehow managed to educate Dick, an engineer for Pratt & Whitney, Tom, a research chemist with Pfizer, and Jack, a clergyman. I was a Coffin, and Coffins are a money-conscious tribe. We'd been given a few pennies for Sunday School as I was growing up. My mother still went each fall to the church fair, enjoyed the turkey dinner, bought an apron or two. So far as I knew, that was the extent of our financial support of organized religion. Clergy depending on Coffin stewardship would certainly have been starved out. So—it took many years to convince me to be truly generous with God. Two legacies helped.

The first came soon after Tom lost his leg and, since plenty of two-legged preachers were available, was asked to retire from active ministry. Methodist clergy, who live in church-owned parsonages, have no place to retire to. Money was badly needed—for medical bills, for an artificial leg, for renting and furnishing a small apartment behind the ***Booklet.***

A letter came from an attorney in Stamford. Charles and Emma Clason had passed away a few months before, had left Tom several thousand dollars . . . The Clasons had been parishioners in Roxbury, the Grenfells' first American church, thirty years before—a long time to remember a clergyman.

The second legacy came a few years later when Ethel was in need, her pension of $9 a week as a minister's widow being not quite sufficient. The same Stamford lawyer wrote again. Mrs. Sarah B. Stevens, the Grenfell boys' first American teacher in Bangall School, Roxbury, had remembered Ethel in her will. Only a few thousand dollars, but enough for Ethel. Not long after her death, I, who had worried about money all my life, decided that I, too, would be generous with God.

The last four years of her life Mother lived on the third floor of our New York City parsonage. There were two other sets of Grenfell grandchildren, but ours were the lucky ones. For Grandma brought into our home the perspective that comes from living close to God for more than seventy years. She had known heartache, homesickness, physical pain, material privation, yet she had taken all with a smile, a joke, with high courage and complete faith in God.

She taught me and my children many things during those years of intimate living. Mainly she taught—and showed—that happiness and money have little to do with each other. "You make your own happiness all along the way" was her philosophy.

I needed a new hat? Let's steam those purple pansies! Lorna has no party dress? That blue velvet's a bit tight on you, dear! Food budget low? Send them up to me. We'll have Cows and Horses, Bubble and Squeak. Cows and Horses was corn syrup on unbuttered bread, but Grandma held the bottle high in the air, dribbled the syrup into queer shapes, shouting loud, excited questions: "Is it a cow? No! Is it a horse? No! It's an elephant!" Bubble and Squeak was yesterday's bit of meat made into hash with boiled potatoes and beets—"Hear it bubble? Hear it squeak?" she'd cry as she pounded the hash. Gales of laughter would float down from the third floor as Ethel showed her loved grandchildren how to have fun, how to 'make their own happiness . . . all along the way.'

And she taught us all to pray. A true Celt, a Druid mystic, her prayers could usher the most sophisticated New York women straight into the presence of God. She disapproved of many things they did—didn't like sherry served at meetings, for instance—but she did not condemn, tried to understand different backgrounds, and she prayed with and for them. Her birthday was February 14, Valentine's Day. On her 77th, four different women, led by Elinora Fleming, brought cakes to the parsonage—many-layered, decorated with hearts, red cherries, her name. People cannot be fooled.

ETHEL WORE SPECTACULAR HATS—TOM WAS NEVER SEEN WITHOUT HIS CLERICAL COLLAR. Here they are on the steps of the Bethel Church, June, 1944, an hour or so after Reverend Tom has christened the granddaughter named for him—Lornagrace Thomas.

When they are truly loved, they know it, and, sophisticated or not, they love back.

This was Ethel's last birthday. "Don't cry when I die!" she had instructed us. "Stand up and sing the ***Hallelujah Chorus.***" We stood up, but no one sang. Margaret Jones played triumphantly on the church organ, but she played from memory—eyes shut tight, face uplifted—and she played on wet keys.

"I think—" John, ten, standing by the graveside in Roxbury, said to the undertaker—"that maybe I'll be a minister when I grow up."

"You children must feel bad," Don Hoskins answered, "seeing your grandmother put into the ground like this."

"Oh, that's not our grandmother," Lorna was quick to reply. "That's just her old worn-out body. It'll prob'ly turn into a rose bush or something." Our children, as I said, were the fortunate ones.

'You must have conflict,' the instructor told our writing class many times. 'You must have conflict, or your writing will be deadly boring.' I hope the story of my mother-in-law has not bored you too much, for there was no conflict. She stood there, that first time, her arms open, saying ***"I love"***— and from then until her last ***"Your loving Mother G,"*** there was no conflict. She was mother-in-law, yes, but she was also mother-in-love.

"In my Father's house are many mansions . . . I go to prepare a place—" He spoke in human terms because we who are human can visualize only in human terms. As I write here in my seventies—father, mother, four brothers, sister, husband all there—the ***"place"*** seems less and less to be dreaded, feared, more and more to be, perhaps, even welcomed. And sometimes I wonder—

Will one of those ***"mansions"*** have many, many climbing roses? and will there be a voice from a doorway, saying ***"I love—"***?

"Bart was waiting on the doorstep . . ." of their first church in New Milford, Connecticut, when the Reverend and Mrs. Jack Grenfell arrived from their honeymoon.

. . . TO LOVE AND TO CHERISH

I take thee to be my wedded husband, to have and to hold, from this day forward, for better, for worse, for richer, for poorer, in sickness and in health, to love and to cherish, till death do us part, according to God's holy ordinance; and thereto I pledge thee my faith.

***"O let us be married!
Too long we have tarried:
But what shall we do for a ring?"***

Edward Lear

CONDOLENCE CALL

Just driving through, *he says,* ***happened to hear***
That she's a widow now . . . so grieved, so sad . . .
But sympathizes . . . lost his own dear wife
Short weeks ago . . .

They sit on the sofa . . . talk . . .
His hand on the empty cushion there between,
Pink palm upturned, pink fingers slightly curled . . .

She knows that hand! Her cheek, her hair, her breast
All know from long ago its tender stroke,
Its lingering, soft caress . . . and now she wants
So much, so very much, to reach across
The sofa cushion there, to feel again
The throb, the pulse, the old familiar touch . . .

She grips her hands together, clenches tight,
The knuckles turning white . . . listens and chats,
Remembers to say thanks for stopping by . . .

And tries to smile, or at least tries not to glare,
At the new wife sitting there in the opposite chair.

ANY FOOL'D KNOW BETTER

"There'll be a little wedding in the parsonage after supper, dear," said the minister casually, feeling important, but trying not to show it.

"After supper!" I gasped. "It's after supper now! When? What time?" I jumped to my feet and started clearing the table.

"Around seven, I think." Rev pulled his appointment book from his pocket and found the right date. "Yes, that's right—seven o'clock."

"It's quarter of now! Why on earth didn't you tell me?" Our own wedding was only a month behind us. The ironstone platter and the wedding presents—we'd been given almost everything except a cook book—had been carefully transported in layers of tissue paper from my old home in Maine to our new home in Connecticut, and even more carefully distributed throughout the ten-room parsonage. With my typewriter, a card file, and the current magazines I'd set about learning to cook something besides fudge and hard-boiled eggs. We'd eaten our way through the July *Good Housekeeping* and the August *McCall's* and were just finishing a fairly tasty salmon loaf from the *Newtown Bee* when Rev made his startling announcement. I thought of Mother's long lists and the months of preparation that had gone into my wedding. Now here was one in my house in less than fifteen minutes! How could Rev sit there calmly eating salmon loaf?

"Why didn't you tell me? Before, I mean?" I took away his coffee cup and blew out the candles.

"My business, dear. Nothing for you to do. What's for dessert?"

"Can't we have it later?" I piled silver and napkins on the tray. "It's cake—no-good, lop-sided, scorched, the-scorch-cut-off, frosted, chocolate cake from the *Danbury News*." I picked up the loaded tray and tottered to the kitchen.

"Hmmm—sounds delicious. You sure that's a Republican paper? Mustn't forget you're from Maine, you know."

"I'm sure it isn't. No Republican paper would print a recipe like that. Where are you going?"

"Have to step over to church for my robe."

"Step ahead." I was crumbing the table fast, and not being a bit particular where the crumbs landed. "Don't mind me."

"Honestly, dear," he stood in the doorway, "parsonage weddings are nothing to get worked up about. They happen all the time. There's no need to fuss. House looks fine. I'll let 'em in." The front door slammed behind him.

No need to fuss! A lot a man knows! My first parsonage wedding and he gives me ten minutes. Just because he's been brought up in a parsonage, he thinks he knows everything. His business, indeed. Guess the way this house looks is my business!

I grabbed yesterday's bouquet of falling phlox from the living-room table and dumped it into the kitchen waste basket. Was there time to wash the dishes?

That was a very sensible parsonage. Next to the kitchen sink were two huge soap-stone wash tubs, mounted on iron pedestals. In one I set the loaded tray of dirty dishes, piled in the other the dozen pots and pans I'd needed to make salmon loaf and chocolate cake, closed the heavy wooden cover and in its exact center casually placed a huge pot of ivy. How was I to know this would become a habit? Months later when the church women asked Rev if there was plenty of room in the parsonage for all our wedding china, his answer puzzled them for days. "Oh, yes," he assured them, "plenty of room—in the set tubs."

I dashed outdoors to pick fresh phlox, filled my biggest wedding-present crystal vase, placed it on the living-room floor between the windows, and ran upstairs to change my dress. I knew, of course, I'd have to be a witness. I didn't know much as yet about being a minister's wife, but I'd seen enough movies to know that. I pulled my best going-away dress off the hanger—navy blue chiffon with white at the neck. *Not going to be one of those horrible creatures Hollywood dreams up, creeping downstairs in the middle of the night in their curl papers and kimono, with a big, toothy grin. . . . Where are my pearls? . . . Darn! There's the bell!*

I took the back stairs—another good feature of this parsonage—three at a time, tiptoed through the kitchen, and stood behind the heavy drapes that separated the dining and living rooms. With my face against the green velvet, I finished fastening my pearls and waited to be called in.

Maybe school teachers can't bake cake, I mused, *but they certainly can hurry—fresh flowers, spotless kitchen (if no one moved the ivy), perfectly groomed wife all in twelve minutes. Bet not every bride can do that. Rev'll be surprised when he calls me in, but when is that going to be?*

More than two pairs of feet were passing along the hall into the living room. In fact, the noise seemed more like a fire drill or Grade 9 coming in from recess. Suddenly I heard an unexpected sound—the sharp, petulant cry of a tiny baby!

Good heavens! Was it that kind of wedding? I stepped back from the drape, expecting a bullet to whiz past my head any moment. *No wonder Rev said this was his business! But what'll I tear up for bandages if somebody gets shot? . . . Not my trousseau sheets!*

The baby's cry was getting louder by the minute. Then a heavy tread advanced down the hall and a cheerful voice recommended, "Give 'im a suck o' the bottle, dearie. That'll shut 'im up." The crying stopped. A satisfied smacking took its place.

"Come right in!" I heard my husband's voice from the porch. "Plenty of room inside for all of you!"

All of you! I marveled. *How many are there? Has the whole clan come to see justice done our Nell?* Indeed, more and more feet were shuffling into the living room. I waited no longer to be called. Opening the green velvet a careful crack, I peeked.

I saw children—children of all ages, all sizes, all stages of being dressed up and dressed down. The tallest girl held the still smacking baby and gathered around her were two, four, six, eight—I gave up counting. Towering over the children, and, in fact, over the whole room, was a great, bubbly mountain of a woman dressed in bright blue lace and putting considerable strain on all twenty yards of it. By her side, looking up at her with dazed admiration, stood a little scrubbed man wearing blue dungarees.

Color matches, I thought, *if the material doesn't. . . . Oh, Rev . . . watch out for my crystal vase!* As the avalanche advanced, the minister was being backed up closer and closer against the pink and white phlox—but not for long. One hungry lad was stuffing fistful after fistful into his mouth. *Give 'im a face full o' phlox, dearie! That'll shut 'im up!*

"Your fourth marriage, madam?" My husband, peering at the license, was using his dignified ministerial tone. "And your first, sir? Well, you're certainly getting a ready-made family! How many of the little—er, ones are there?" Here the minister bent down, pulled phlox-eater out of the big vase, and handed him, coughing violently, to the second tallest girl.

"Got eleven," beamed Blue Lace in the same sunny voice that had prescribed for the howling baby. "Well, no," she amended, doubtless feeling strictest honesty was called for when speaking to a member of the clergy. "Eleven and two-thirds, really. There's another one comin' 'round Thanksgivin'."

No one, looking at the expanding network of blue lace, would have thought of questioning this prediction, but the bridegroom seemed to feel the need of a word of explanation.

"Took awful sudden, her last one was, Revrunt. 'Bout a month ago, if you recall that bad storm. But she needs a man powerful bad—'round the farm, that is—so we—"

"Act o' God," pronounced Blue Lace. Delighted to have found a subject of common theological interest with the new minister, she elaborated. "Act o' God, they called it at the fun'rul. He wuz struck down by lightnin', Revrunt, on his way to milk the cows. Stood under the but'nut tree, so's he wouldn't git soaked to the skin, and do you know the lightnin' skun the bark—"

"Killed him dead," summarized Blue Dungars, obviously feeling it was time to swing the spotlight to the new lead. But Blue Lace was not to be swung so easily.

". . . skun the bark right off'n that but'nut tree, Revrunt. Killed him dead." The Revrunt, trying to look sympathetic for the dead and at the same time joyful for the living, pulled from beneath his black robes another little runt who'd been busy skinning the bark off *his* shins. He handed him to the third tallest girl. Blue Lace rambled cozily on.

". . . now wouldn't you think, Revrunt, that any fool'd know better'n to stand under a but'nut tree in a thunderstorm? Why, my ma always told all us kids, and her ma before 'er, 'Now, don't *none* o' you young'uns ever stand—' "

"Stand right over here, please." The Revrunt, who'd been standing for some time with his book open to ***Order for the Solemnization of Matrimony,*** motioned Blue Dungars to the right of the Blue Ridge Mountain. "And may I have the ring?"

"Golly Ned!" Blue Dungars' dazed admiration turned to dazed distress. "Would ya believe it, Revrunt, I wuz so dang busy cleaning out the cows and cleaning up the kids, I clean fergot the ring?"

But Blue Lace, an old hand at matrimony, had everything under control. "Got one right here," she beamed, reaching over to break the twine string around the baby's neck and pry from his fist a thick gold band. "Always use the same one—for kids and husbands. Ain't nuthin'll bring a young'un's tooth through quicker'n bitin' down on a solid gold ring. Better remember that, Revrunt," she added coyly. "Heard you jist got hitched yourself!"

Blue Lace gave the dented band a vigorous swipe across the wide expanse of her left hip and handed to the minister what was undoubtedly the most utilitarian wedding ring in America. "Here 'tis—all shined up and good as new."

The minister, looking almost as dazed as did Blue Dungars at this demonstration of New England economy, laid the ring carefully on the open page of his ***Ritual*** and opened his mouth to begin.

"Dearly—"

"Wow!" screamed the infant, suddenly putting his fist to his gums and discovering the loss of his teething ring.

". . . beloved—"

"Wow! Wow! Wow!" Fifteen pounds of red, writhing indignation expressed itself without inhibition. For the first time Blue Lace's composure seemed shaken. She swung around quickly toward the source of the trouble, upsetting, all in one mighty motion, book, ring, and what was left of the vase of phlox.

"Give 'im a suck o' the bottle, dearie!" But a minor catastrophe had developed. The bottle was empty. "Where's another bottle?" The mother looked severely down into the sea of upturned faces. "Didn't none o' you kids bring along another bottle?"

None of you kids had. Suddenly Second Tallest dropped Phlox-Eater on the floor. "I know where there's one, Ma—out in the truck. But it's only half-full!"

"Fetch it," ordered Blue Lace. "Weddings don't take long. There, there," she crooned, as Blue Dungars on his hands and knees tracked down the ring and the Revrunt wiped phlox water off his ***Ritual,*** "there's somethin' comin' soon for the little darlin'." Indeed, Second Tallest was back with the bottle. Giving the nipple a swipe across her right hip, Blue Lace stuck it hastily into the open mouth. "Now mind," she admonished Tallest, "poke it to 'im good if he bellers. Can't have no bellerin' in the service."

The audience fanned back as Blue Lace faced front again, and the minister put his hand over the ring. Blue Lace reached down once more and took the groom's gnarled fist into her own capable grasp. "O.K., Revrunt," she smiled, her sunny self again. "Get goin', 'fore he empties the bottle."

Witness—I closed the crack in the drapes and crept up the back stairs to take off my chiffon dress—*All those two need is baby-sitters, and they've got a built-in supply for the next twenty years.*

I gave the dishes an extra scalding, because of the set tubs, and was hanging the towels on the line in the back yard when my husband came down the steps. He handed me a small, white envelope.

"What's this?" I asked coldly, determined not to show the slightest interest in *his* business. After all, he might have told me he was marrying a widow with eleven offspring.

"For you. Open it." I opened it and saw green.

"For me?" I was astounded. I had thought my days of free, unaccounted-for cash were over. "You mean I get the wedding fees?"

"Not fees. Honorariums. Gifts. Don't you know anything about the church? ***'We will on no account make any charge—'*** "

"Five dollars!" I gloated. "I saw the darlingest hat—"

"You're learning fast. The minister's wife always gets the little envelopes, and she always buys big, floppy hats—"

"But that poor little man!" I suddenly remembered. "And all those children! And another one comin' 'round the mountain—I mean, comin' 'round Thanksgiving!"

The Reverend kissed the back of my neck as I hung up the last towel. "I'm glad you said that. I'd have given it back if this hadn't been your first. Sort of wanted you to have the first." I turned around so he wouldn't have to kiss the back of my neck. The forsythia bushes around our back yard grew very high.

"But how did you know about the 'poor little man'?" my husband asked after awhile. "And the Thanksgiving arrival? Of course, teachers have eyes in the back of their head, but can they see through green velvet?"

"Through the crack . . . I was sure I'd be a witness . . . I put on my best going-away dress . . . waited for you to call—"

"Silly . . . don't you know witnesses aren't required in Connecticut?"

"I do now."

"Well, then—how about a piece of lopsided, burned, shaved-off, Democratic chocolate cake?"

"You know," I said, as we climbed the back steps together, "maybe I won't buy a big, floppy hat this first time. Maybe I'll buy a big, floppy cook book." And I did.

GIVEN BY THE CHURCHES THEY SERVED, family, and friends, the pulpit in the new United Methodist Church in Darien, Connecticut, honors three generations of Grenfell clergymen "for the inspiration, comfort, and challenge of their preaching:

THOMAS . . . who began and ended his ministry in America within a few miles of the Darien parish.

JACK . . . who as pastor, 1964-1968, led in capturing the vision, acquiring the site, and planning the architecture of this new building.

*JOHN MILLARD . . . who was ordained by Bishop Lloyd C. Wicke in 1968, the first member of this church to enter the Christian ministry."**

**From the Order of Worship, Dedication Sunday, March 14, 1971, Darien, Connecticut.*

"What good are Latin? German? Greek? French?" Clarine asked as she tried to cook, sew, and iron starched shirts for her minister husband. Here they are at Hartford Theological Seminary the day they received Bachelor of Divinity degrees, May 28, 1938, one month before their marriage.

. . . WITH THIS RING I THEE WED

The wedding ring is the outward and visible sign of an inward and spiritual grace, signifying to all the uniting of this man and this woman in holy matrimony through the Church of Jesus Christ our Lord. Bless, O Lord, the giving of this ring, that he who gives it and she who wears it may abide forever in thy peace, and continue in thy favor; through Jesus Christ our Lord.
Amen.

In token and pledge of our constant faith and abiding love, with this ring I thee wed, in the name of the Father, and of the Son, and of the Holy Spirit. Amen.

"Love alone is capable of uniting living beings in such a way as to complete and fulfill them, for it alone takes them and joins them by what is deepest in themselves."

Pierre Teilhard de Chardin

LIGHTLY IN FALL

Lightly in fall a red clay path they trod,
Crossed brittle fields, then climbed a hill to find
A high cathedral in the lofty pines . . .
Talked there awhile of poems and God and things
Until the lifeblood of the dying day
Stained the green needles of the murmuring choir,
Then homeward turned, and knew that they were one—
One in the crimson of the dying day . . .
One in the harmony of swaying trees . . .
One in the muffled heartbeat of the dusk . . .

They spoke few words, and hand had scarce touched hand,
Yet with a passion half-divine they knew
That far beyond the sunset's reddest hue
Their trembling souls lay one upon God's breast—
Knew, and did not care about the rest.

Hartford Theological Seminary

Eighty-ninth Annual Session
The New York East Conference
of the
Methodist Episcopal Church

IN SESSION AT
Hanson Place Central Church
Hanson Place and St. Felix Street, Brooklyn, N. Y.
MAY 11 - 17, 1937

HANSON PLACE CENTRAL CHURCH

Clarine, Darling --

I am being ordained tonight, as you know, Darling, but it's not just me being ordained -- it's us! I know it is! I am giving myself to the greatest cause on earth -- the Gospel of Jesus Christ -- but it is not just me. You are by my side. We are one.

I am being placed in the hands of the Church tonight, but I know it is not only my body, but a Spirit composed of two hearts that are beating as one and are ready to go anywhere and serve for their Master. I am happy. I am glad. I am not alone. I never shall be alone, for with me is the heart that is mine, the soul that is mine, and she has with her my heart and soul.

I thank God this evening for her who right now is thinking of and praying for me, even as I am praying for her.

May God bless us and cause His face to shine upon us and give peace.

I love you.

Jack

Jack

THE METHODIST CHURCH turned down Clarine's request for ordination—was not to ordain women clergy for another twenty years. Jack understood her feeling of rejection. She calls this her 'Letter of Ordination.'

KNOWLEDGE

I would know your lips
though I could see no face . . .

would know your arms
ten thousand years from now . . .

would know your voice,
though it called through endless space . . .

would know and come to you . . .
somewhere, somehow . . . .

THE LITTLE ENVELOPE

"What earthly good is it?" I unpinned my Phi Beta Kappa key with the tips of my fingers and tossed it into the jewel box. "Something is wrong with American education. Not going to wear it again till I can fry a decent batch of doughnuts."

"Doughnuts?" Rev stuck his head out of the closet where he was examining the row of white shirts I'd spent the morning ironing. "Where?" he asked expectantly.

"In the garbage can. As usual." I was counting my blisters—six red ones from the doughnut fat, two watery white ones from the hot iron. They all hurt. "Honestly, Rev, I'm so discouraged. I can't cook. I can't sew. I can't wash—"

"You can't iron collars," Rev picked up the theme. He dumped a dozen shirts on the bed and started pulling them off the hangers. "Have to hurry. Laundry closes at six."

Around his neck was a bright red rash an inch wide. The week before I'd starched his collars stiff as a board. This week I'd cut down on the starch and the shirts hung like dish rags. I came over and started to help him unbutton all the little buttons I'd spent half my morning buttoning onto the hangers.

"I'll do it." He was looking at my blisters. "Sorry, honey, but the Gower wedding's tomorrow. Collar has to look right, if nothing else does." I knew what he meant. I'd pressed his trousers, too, on the seams. I sat down on the bed, fingering a limp shirt tail.

"They're nice and white," I said brightly. "Did you notice? I used lots of Chlorox in the first rinse."

"Oh? By the way, what happened to my pajamas? Noticed 'em on the line as I came in."

"Rev, do you think you should wear bright red pajamas? Are they suitable, I mean, for a minister?"

"Variegated pink is better?" He was counting his shirts. Somehow he seemed to lose a few each time I washed. "—nine, ten, eleven—where's my Van Heusen?" The Van Heusen was his best shirt. He'd bought it for our honeymoon.

"I—I don't suppose you ever have occasion to wear a variegated pink shirt?"

He stopped unbuttoning and looked at me. "Oh, no!"

"Oh, yes. I'm sorry, Rev. It—it sort of got mixed up with the red pajamas and the Chlorox."

He shook his head and went back to his buttons. "Save it for Christmas. Maybe they'll want me to be Santa Claus."

"I tried to make Yorkshire pudding, like your mother's, to—to make up for the shirt. But I couldn't."

"Not in your American cook book?"

"Oh, the recipe's there, but it calls for 'shortening,' and I still can't find out what the stuff is. You sure you don't know?"

"Never heard of it. Why don't you just order some and see what you get?"

"I tried to, today, and Uncle Henry wanted to know what kind. What could I say—pasteurized? pink? granulated? liquid? How do I know what kind I want when I don't even know what it is?"

"What *did* you say?"

"Said I guessed I had enough to last me for awhile—not to bother. Wish I knew, though. Dictionary says it makes pastry crisp and light, and more 'n half the recipes call for it." I handed Rev the last shirt. The brown print of the iron was over the breast pocket. That's when I'd gotten my biggest blister. He handed it back to me.

"Not worth paying the laundry. And you know very well how to find out what shortening is. Ask any of the church women."

"And be laughed at even more? They're still hilarious over my cake—and so are you," I accused. He had disappeared into the closet, shoulders shaking. He came back.

"You—you looked so darn proud, darlin', carrying that three-layer cake across the church lawn and then, when the top layer slid—"

"I know," I interrupted coldly. "I was the one who had to kneel down and pick it out of the grass. Notice you didn't rush over to help."

"Toothpicks—" he was still convulsed. "Mrs. Rydell sent you toothpicks."

"Half the women in the church sent me toothpicks. We've got toothpicks enough for layer cakes for the rest of our lives. If they have food sales every day and Sunday, we've still got enough."

Rev wiped his eyes and his glasses on the burned shirt. "You don't *have* to bake for church food sales."

"Of course I do. I'm the minister's wife, remember? Wish I could fry doughnuts. That'd show 'em. But every batch is greasier than the one before."

"Shapes are interesting, though." Rev gave my shape a friendly whack as he gathered up the empty hangers.

"Why is it so hard to make holes? You'd think any moron could make little round empty holes! I'm starving for something fit to eat and I can't cook it. Rev, why didn't I take home ec? What good are Latin? German? Greek? French?"

"Maybe you should've bought a French cook book." His bundle of shirts under his arm, Rev made an exaggerated bow from the doorway. "'*Let me kees your han', madame, your bleestered fingah teeps, madame*—' Here's Uncle Henry now. Keep trying, honey. I'm sort of hungry, too."

I trailed him dejectedly down the stairs. Like most newlyweds, we were having money troubles. Our salary was twenty-five dollars a week, and we budgeted five for food. This would have been enough in 1938 if I'd known how to cook the food after we bought it, but I didn't. Half my efforts went straight to the garbage can, not the table. I'd even spent my five wedding envelopes for food—"Ministers' wives always get the little envelopes," Rev had told me, handing me my first one, "and they always buy big, floppy hats." Not this minister's wife! I'd bought a cook book with the first one, and food to practice on ever since. I'd spent nineteen years of my life going to school and four more teaching school, but, when it came to living, I didn't seem to know anything. *Anyone except Rev,* I thought, *would have tossed me out long ago.*

The carton of groceries was on the kitchen table, but Uncle Henry had gone. He was in his seventies, but hopped on and off his delivery truck like a teenager. I started unpacking the food—

"Rev," I called out the window, "did you order a honeydew melon? There's one here . . . or a can of chicken?"

"No! Call him up!" He backed out the drive, interested in shirts, not groceries.

"You've made a mistake in our order," I told Uncle Henry over the phone. "There's a honeydew melon here, but I didn't order one, and a can of boned chicken."

"On your bill?" Uncle Henry asked grumpily and banged the receiver in my ear. I looked at the pink slip. Neither melon nor chicken was listed. He's getting old, I thought. He makes mistakes, but he doesn't want to admit them.

Once or twice again I called Uncle Henry when things I hadn't ordered appeared in our carton. He always asked the same question—"On your bill?"—and he always hung up on me. "This has got to stop," I told Rev one Saturday as I unpacked the weekend groceries. "The old man is mixing orders two or three times a week. He's losing money. I ordered cold cuts for tomorrow, and they're here, but look what was under them!" I held up a ten-pound ham.

"Be nice to have ham," said Rev wistfully. "I think it's easy, too. You do something with pineapple."

So the next morning before church I decorated the ham with pineapple slices and put it in the oven, but after the service I waited for Uncle Henry.

"Good morning," I said, as he and his wife came along. "Uncle Henry, we want to pay you—"

"Mornin'," growled Uncle Henry, glaring at me fiercely. "Nice mornin'." He pushed past me down the church steps, dragging his wife behind him.

"Good morning, dear," she called back over her shoulder.

So we went home and ate the ham. For even I (who had never lived in a parsonage before and was quite unprepared for the many ways a minister is loved by his people) had finally gotten it through my head that Uncle Henry was not making mistakes.

He was teaching me the care and feeding of ministers. Lesson for the day: cold cuts, no matter how easy, are not the right Sunday dinner for a man who pours out his heart in the pulpit Sunday morning. Extra items continued to appear in our carton—protein when he thought we needed more protein, and fruit when he thought I hadn't ordered enough fruit—until the day Uncle Henry sold his grocery store and retired. On that day he lined our pantry shelves with food for weeks to come.

Other donations often appeared on our back steps. Almost everyone in the parish had a garden—large or small—and many weeks when the five food dollars were gone and there had been no wedding envelope, an anonymous bag of peas or corn or eggplant would tide us over until pay day. We seldom knew whom to thank for these offerings, but Rev happened to be home the Saturday Mrs. Rydell brought gourds.

"What are they?" I asked when he showed them to me. "Little squashes? Dwarf pumpkins?" I had just found out about dwarf tomatoes and was feeling quite agricultural.

"Gourds, silly. Didn't you ever read the Bible? They use 'em around Thanksgiving."

I searched my cook book to learn how to prepare this Biblical Thanksgiving food, but I could find no recipe for gourds. The next day before church, I waylaid Mrs. Rydell in the choir room.

"Thank you for the lovely gourds," I told her, and all the choir members stopped talking out of courtesy to the little new minister's wife. "Tell me," I said into the silence, "how do you make your gourd pie?"

The anthem that morning was ***'the shocks of corn, they laugh and sing,'*** and it was a good thing, because the choir shook all the while they were singing. Frankly, I never did understand what was so hilarious. In Maine, where I come from, we don't grow stuff for nothing. But Mrs. Rydell came the next day with a brush and a can of orange shellac and showed me how to paint gourds. We used them for years as our Thanksgiving centerpiece—and, Rev, of course, always apologized to our guests because I hadn't had time to make my famous gourd pie.

So, gradually, with infinite love and teasing affection, the laconic New Milford parish educated the two innocent babes in the parsonage; for, in many ways, the man of the house was just as deficient as the woman.

Rev 'fixed' the toaster, so that only one side of the bread ever

browned. He repaired the washing machine, and it never drained again. He re-wired old lamps that promptly blew new fuses. But by far the worst drain on our pocketbook was the car.

Our parish was the longest in Connecticut—eighteen miles, as the crow flies, but many more than eighteen as Rev pushed our fourth-hand Dodge up and down the Berkshire hills to make his parish calls. There was always something wrong with the car. Right now it was the brakes.

"Got to be re-lined," he announced gloomily. He had stopped at the garage on his way back from the laundry. "Going to be expensive."

"How much?" I was stirring a white sauce for the boned chicken.

"Maybe twenty-five." He sliced off a wedge of melon.

"Perhaps there'll be twenty-five tomorrow, in the little envelope." We had never had a twenty-five-dollar wedding, or even a twenty-dollar one, but I was feeling optimistic. My blisters had stopped smarting, the white sauce hadn't lumped, and I had already enjoyed half the honey dew. "Laura Gower's fiance looks like a nice man."

"He is a nice man, but don't you start counting chickens . . . Laura's not bad either," he grinned. "I hear she's quite a cook."

"She's beautiful," I agreed, refusing to be teased.

The next day as I watched her come slowly down the aisle in white satin, I said the same thing again under my breath, for Laura Gower was one of the loveliest brides my husband ever married. A shapely brunette with a sweet face and brown eyes soft as pansies, she was everyone's dream of what a bride should be. The minister's collar—stiff, white, and fresh from the laundry—looked nice, too.

I told him so, as we sped over the tortuous dirt roads to the reception—the Gowers lived eight miles from church—but he was worrying about brakes and paid no attention.

"Hang on," he shouted, pumping up and down on the useless

pedal. I hung on for dear life as we swung around a curve and scraped a chicken fence. Two dozen hens rose indignantly into the air behind us.

"How much was in the envelope?" I called above the cackling.

"Don't have it yet . . . besides, you know I never open it." We were starting down an even steeper hill. I closed my eyes and saw the headlines in tomorrow's paper—

LOCAL CLERGYMAN, YOUNG WIFE
KILLED INSTANTLY ON WAY TO—

"Open it this time!" I screamed. "Buy brakes! Let's hope it'll be enough!"

Two hours later as we backed out of the Gower drive we still didn't have the little envelope. The best man came running after us.

"Almost forgot," he grinned. The reception had been fun, Laura and her nice man had left in a swirl of confetti, and Rev himself with pink and green sprinkled all over his black Homburg looked quite rakish.

"Thanks!" Rev waved, and handed me the envelope. We started down the sharp incline for home. "Open it," he ordered. "Take out your twenty-five dollars. And sit closer."

I moved as close as possible and carefully tore the edge of the little envelope. I pulled out five fresh green pictures of Abraham Lincoln.

"It is! It is!" I cried, swinging around and waving them in his astonished face. "It's twenty-five dollars! . . . Oh, Rev! Watch out! Stop! Step on the brakes!"

But there weren't any brakes, to speak of, to step on, and I had jerked his arm and cut off his vision, and we stopped at last bang up against a Connecticut stone wall.

The bill for the radiator—Rev found a second-hand one in the automobile graveyard—came to $24.95. So we had had a twenty-five-dollar wedding, and we had cleared exactly a nickel. We still didn't have any brakes.

"Going to put 'em in myself." Rev walked through the kitchen a few days later carrying what looked like four pieces of stiff, grey ribbon. "Bought the new linings. Garageman told me just how to install 'em. It's the labor that costs," he added wisely, slamming the screen door.

Remembering the washing machine and the toaster, I had my doubts, but I kept still. Somehow the things we did to save money always seemed to cost more than the things we wanted to buy in the first place. It was reasonable to suppose that a man who could discuss eschatology and existentialism for hours on end could follow a garageman's simple instructions for putting a grey ribbon on a brake, but still—the recipe for doughnuts looks easy, too.

Rev stayed on his back under the car all morning. I admired his persistence, if nothing else, and out of sympathy for his prostrate position got down on my own knees and scrubbed the kitchen floor. He emerged at noon, covered with grease from head to foot, long enough for a sandwich and a glass of lemonade, and crawled back under. I could tell by his silence that things weren't going too well. Around three I handed him another glass of lemonade. He just reached out one black paw and took it. He didn't even say thanks.

I was looking up 'Brakes' in the encyclopedia when I heard the doorbell. Probably a probationer, I thought, hurrying downstairs. Rev was probation officer for the town, and everyone the judge put 'on probation' had to report to the parsonage once a week that all was well. Now and then all was not well. The week before an alcoholic gentleman had been reporting how well everything was when a fifth of Scotch slipped out from under his jacket and smashed on the hall floor. I'd wiped it up, but that afternoon the ladies had sniffed all during the missionary meeting.

"Is the minister in?" the man asked pleasantly. I noted the deep, healthy tan and faded chinos. Not a probationer, I decided. More likely a farmer.

"He's in the back yard, working on the car. Shall I call him?"

"Don't bother," he smiled. "I'll just go 'round." I went back to ***Britannica,*** wishing all the probationers were as nice as this farmer in faded chinos. But a few minutes later when Rev stormed in the back door, he was far from pleased.

"You might have asked him in, and called me! Given me a chance to get some of the grease off—"

I looked up, startled. He'd never used quite that tone before.

"I'm sorry—"

"Covered with muck from head to foot—" he turned on the kitchen faucet full blast and reached for the cleanser. "Couldn't even shake hands!"

"I'm sorry," I said, a little louder. "Was it someone important? I thought—"

"Anyone! Does it matter?" He was spraying more water and shaking more cleanser on my clean floor than on his dirty hands.

But two can shout as well as one.

"Who was it?"

"Tell 'em to come in! Ask 'em to sit down! Come get me! Give *them* a glass of lemonade!—"

"I know what to do! My mother brought me up right! We kept an old Emily Post in the bathroom! Now who is he, and why doesn't he buy some new pants?"

"Pants?" asked Rev, in a perfectly friendly voice. "What's wrong with his pants? And what's wrong with you, dear? You're screeching like a fish wife."

"Who is he?" I whispered hoarsely.

"That man? Oh, Arthur Krock. Wants me to marry him tomorrow."

"Here?" My voice, too, was perfectly normal again. I was always interested in a wedding.

"No. At a summer place, five miles out."

"But how'll you get there? Is the car done?" I knew very well it wasn't, else he wouldn't have been in such a temper.

"Well—almost . . . got a rag to wipe off this grease?"

I pulled the pink Van Heusen out of the rag bag and handed it to him. "Call the garage," I said. "Ask them to finish the job. Mr. Krock writes for the *New York Times*. He's bound to give me a fat little envelope. My treat, darling—for forgetting my parsonage manners."

"Thank you," said the minister grandly. "I accept." With hands still grimy, he picked up the phone.

Giving him the envelope was really no sacrifice on my part. The meals had all been fairly edible that week, and as for hats—by that time I had learned to switch roses and gardenias and daisies with safety pins underneath, and make one big, floppy hat go a long, long way. Besides, I was extremely allergic to Connecticut stone walls.

My British husband, I was finding out, was somewhat like a Connecticut stone wall himself in many ways, especially where the church was concerned. He had convictions that couldn't be budged for love or money—especially money. No matter how welcome the little envelopes would have been at certain times, he still turned couples away. The blessing of the church must not be given to any who seemed to be taking marriage vows too casually. Envelopes—frequent and fat, or few and lean—were only incidental and influenced his decisions not at all. I learned this first from the girl who wanted to be married at one minute past midnight in the tavern.

She rang our bell a few days after the Krock wedding, and if the faded chinos of the famous Washington journalist had been misleading, so was her face. She looked like an angel, but her request was along more secular lines. The minister was out, so I invited her to come in and sit down. I even offered lemonade, but she didn't seem too interested.

Would the Reverend, she wondered, stop by the tavern about midnight Saturday (well, Sunday morning, really) long enough to marry her?

I must have looked puzzled, for she went on to explain. The license wouldn't be valid until Sunday (they'd sort of forgotten to get it) and they'd figured they could save a whole day on their honeymoon (only had two weeks) if they invited all their friends (*love* to have me come, too) down to the tavern Saturday night for the party, and then stopped for a few minutes at 12:01 (that would be Sunday morning, and the license would be O.K.) just long enough for the Reverend to tie the knot (it didn't take very long, did it?) if he would be so kind?

The Reverend wouldn't.

I had relayed the angelic message faithfully, along with a more earthly message of my own—the five dollars were all spent, no one had left a bag, and Uncle Henry was away on vacation.

Still, the Reverend wouldn't, and didn't.

But another clergyman in town would, and did.

"So what difference did it make?" I asked. I knew Uncle Henry wouldn't approve, but I was serving Maine flap-jacks, the cheapest thing I could think of, for Sunday dinner. Rev played with the label on the bottle of imitation Vermont maple syrup and didn't answer.

"What did it matter?" I asked again. "They got married anyway. We could have bought another ham! Weren't you just being stuffy?"

"Dearly beloved," he quoted softly, ***"we are gathered together here, in the sight of these beer mugs . . ."***

"Oh, all right," I kissed the top of his head as I put flap-jacks and margarine before him. "You've got standards . . . A juke box isn't an organ."

"Right . . . and a brass rail isn't an altar rail." He reached across the table and took my hand. The red blisters had faded. The white ones were nearly healed.

"Sorry you married me?" he asked, his finger on my wedding ring.

I shook my head. "No—"

"I have to give it His blessing, you know. It's not a sacrament, of course, but it is a sacred rite . . . a part of creation—on-going creation . . ."

I blinked back foolish tears and smiled across the flap-jacks at my minister.

"I know," I said. "Stop explaining." With hands still joined, we bowed our heads—for His blessing.

REV MARRIED HUNDREDS of couples. Joan Reiss and Peter Melrose, organist at South Park Church in Hartford, were two of his favorite young people.

THE FOUR-STOREYED VICTORIAN MONSTROSITY Clarine readied for Marian Anderson's wedding.

Forasmuch as this man and this woman have consented together in holy wedlock, and have witnessed the same before God and this company, and thereto have pledged their faith each to the other and have declared the same by joining hands and giving and receiving rings; I pronounce that they are husband and wife together, in the name of the Father, and of the Son, and of the Holy Spirit. Those whom God hath joined together let not man put asunder.
Amen.

"Music arose with its voluptuous swell,
Soft eyes look'd love to eyes which spake again,
And all went merry as a marriagė bell."

Lord Byron

WORDS, LONG AFTER

For Nancy Morse Dysart, who arranges such things . . .

So we meet on a summer night as the music plays
At a place where the music played long years ago . . .
A place where we danced at a ball long years ago . . .
"Isn't this nice!" *you say, guiding our steps*
Along shadowed walks across the patio,
Old people, moving cautiously and slow . . .
Then, pride in your voice, ***"I want you to meet my son!"***

I see a smiling man, a face I know . . .
Dark eyes alight with whimsey, wit . . . the same
Lopsided grin I traced with fingertips
As we laughed and loved at a ball long years ago . . .
As you whispered words at a ball long years ago . . .
"Your father sent me your picture once," *I say,*
"On a Christmas card . . . was it thirty years ago?
You were wearing your Dr. Denton's—"
I hold out my hand . . .

But echoing there in the night are other words,
Words heard as the music played long years ago . . .
Words heard as you held me close long years ago . . .
'I can't imagine anyone else but you
Mother of my children—no one else but you . . . .'

Now your son holds my hand, and I look at him,
longing to say:
"Come close! Oh, please—do you know me? I am the one—
Let me touch your face!—the one who might have been . . ."

But he drops my hand, for he does not know, and have you
Forgotten, too, words said when all was new:
'I can't imagine anyone else but you—'?
Words said as the music played long years ago . . .
Words said as we danced at a ball long years ago . . .
As I danced in your arms at a ball long years ago . . . .

SOMEHOW I ALWAYS THOUGHT

Somehow I always thought you'd come again . . .
One winter day, perhaps—I'd see you stride
Across some crowded airport, bag in hand,
Eyes searching till you found me, or some spring
You'd swing into my drive, sit grinning there
Behind the wheel till I flung wide the door
And bade you in . . . somehow I always thought . . .

Somehow I always thought you'd come again . . .
In summertime or some bright day in fall . . .
We'd walk and talk and laugh and go again
To places that we knew and know again
The peace and joy not ever known elsewhere . . .

Somehow I always thought—until today.
Your name, your face here on the page . . . long list
Of great accomplishments, all duly praised,
The many things you did all eulogized,
All known, all noted here . . . except for two—
The two I knew . . .
                    you loved me, went away,
And did not, will not ever, come again.

'DEO VOLENTE . . . PLEASE —'

Today we closed the camp—pulled in the float,
Beached boats, stacked paddles, oars, stored fishing poles,
Dug dahlia bulbs against the killing frost,
Drained pipes, capped chimney tops, swept clean the hearth,
Then groped our way, the windows shuttered tight,
Through darkened, silent rooms, and turned the key.

Today we closed the camp—did once again
Chores done together now year after year,
Chatted and teased, yet each was wondering who—
Each asking the unspoken question, who—
Come spring would fling these bolted shutters wide?
Who kneel to light new fires? launch boats at dawn,
Cast for the wary trout? who dive from the float?
Swim lazily face up to noonday sun,
To white, unmoving clouds? or paddle out
Halfway across the lake in inky black
To wait the rising moon, to hear loons call,
To drift, to gaze at stars . . . and who—oh, who—
Would plant these shriveled bulbs to bloom again?

Today we closed the camp—each silently
Asking the question, answering silently:
'Let it be us! ***. . . Deo volente*** *. . . please—*
Another spring let it still be you and me . . . .'

THE 'INSIDE' STORY

'Not even Julie . . .'

NEW YORK CALLING: Mrs. Grenfell? Is your husband white or black?

BOSTON CALLING: We have a rumor your husband married Marian Anderson—

PHILADELPHIA CALLING: Was she married in a church? Did she wear white satin?

BALTIMORE CALLING: Is Marian Anderson married? Did your husband—?

There was an 'inside' story of Marian Anderson's wedding. It happened inside a Connecticut parsonage.

The phone started ringing sometime after midnight, one Friday in late November. Rev was in New York, picking up some last-minute carpeting that couldn't be delivered. For two years he'd been rebuilding the Bethel church. The job was done at last, and a bishop was coming to dedicate it.

John woke me in his usual way, standing by my bed, pulling up my eyelids. "Phone, Mommy—phone, Mommy—phone—" John was only two, but even he knew the parsonage phone must always be answered.

"Thanks, darlin'. Go back to bed." I stumbled downstairs. Must be something important, or they'd have hung up long ago.

NEW YORK CALLING:

"Hello . . . No, he's in New York . . . yes, this is she."

"Mrs. Grenfell? Is your husband white or black?"

What joker was this at one o'clock in the morning? "Sort of tanned, the last time I saw him. Who's this?" He named his paper. By morning my head was a jumble of ***News, Heralds, Banners, Stars, Times.***

"We have reason to think your husband married Miss Marian Anderson last summer. Would you confirm that, please."

"Sorry. I don't discuss Mr. Grenfell's work."

"Just say 'yes' or 'no'. Is Miss Anderson married? We know she took out a license in your town. Did your husband marry her?"

"Why don't you ask Miss Anderson?"

"She's on the West Coast . . . can't be reached. Now, Mrs. Grenfell, you must know about this—"

"Goodnight—"

"Don't hang up! We'll pay you—"

"Sorry." I stumbled upstairs. ***Press isn't so smart,*** I thought. ***It's taken them four months.***

Five minutes later I was stumbling down again.

PHILADELPHIA CALLING: "Is Marian Anderson married? Was it a church wedding? Did she wear white satin? We'll pay you—"

"Sorry—" Back to bed. Down again.

BOSTON CALLING: "We have a rumor . . ."

NEW YORK AGAIN: "Where does your husband usually stay in the city, Mrs. Grenfell? Which hotel? . . . You're sure you can't tell us where to find—Don't hang up! We'll pay—"

Back to bed. Down again. This time I brought a pillow and a blanket.

BALTIMORE CALLING: "Is Marian Anderson married . . .?"

I lay down on the sofa beside the telephone. It rang off and on all night while I reviewed college journalism courses and the geography of the Atlantic seaboard. I wished Rev were home. I wished he'd told me where he'd be staying. He'd know how to handle this. Had we kept Miss Anderson's secret long enough? Should I tell them and get some sleep? New baby coming in two months . . . old Bishop coming in two days . . .

I didn't even consider taking the phone off the hook. The first thing a parsonage wife learns is the importance of the telephone. Life, birth, death—one never knows what is waiting on the other end of the line. Besides, this was 1943, a war year. Boys from our little town were in uniform all over the world. Helen Shaw's tragic words had come over the phone only a short time before—"Can

Rev come? . . . telegram . . . Saipan." Her Bill—handsome, laughing, eighteen years old—had joined the Marines and begged to see action. No, the parsonage phone must always be answered, sleep or no sleep.

Minnie Stryker stopped by the next morning to help dust for the Bishop. As usual when a parsonage baby is on the way, the whole parish was babying the minister's wife. Minnie found me asleep on the sofa and John sharing a stale doughnut with the neighbor's dog. She put oatmeal on to cook for John, put me to bed, and put in a call for Yorke Finger to come sit by the phone. "No comment," I told her sleepily. "Just tell them 'No comment.'"

Rev burst in at three with rolls of wine carpeting under each arm.

"Did I do right?" I asked. "Should I have told them? Shall I tell them now?" The calls had lessened as the day wore on, but there was still an occasional one. I didn't know then, but the story was to break coast-to-coast in the evening papers. Marian Anderson in 1943 was very big news, indeed.

"Say nothing." Rev was pawing through his tool box. "Let Miss Anderson tell her own story. What have you done with the hammer?" He dashed out. Carpet must be tacked for Bishop to walk on. Mustn't trip coming down the aisle. He'd be doing just that in a very few hours.

There were big headlines in the evening papers: ***WORLD-FAMED CONTRALTO SECRETLY MARRIED LAST JULY . . . MARIAN ANDERSON WEDS CHILDHOOD SWEETHEART*** . . . Then in much smaller type, ***". . . officiating clergyman, the Reverend Jack Grenfell, pastor of the Methodist Church in Bethel, Connecticut."***

Such were the simple facts of Miss Anderson's story. Reporters called for days, offering fabulous sums for what they called 'the inside story.' My husband simply said there wasn't any.

I couldn't smile then, to hear him say that, but I can now. For there was an 'inside' story, a rather poignant little 'inside' story—of love and foolish pride and disappointment. Miss Anderson knew nothing about it, and newspapers would not have been interested, for it was really an 'inside-the-parsonage' story. Perhaps, here in 1983, their 40th anniversary year, Mr. and Mrs. Orpheus Fisher will smile, too, if I tell it.

I was on the floor, patching John's overalls, when Rev came in. It was July. It was hot. I was pregnant. The floor was the coolest place.

"Where's that Marian Anderson record?" He went straight to the phonograph.

"Halfway down the pile . . . it's almost worn out. Wish we could buy a new one."

He let the needle down carefully. The tender tones of that beautiful, controlled voice cried out to me, as they always did. I let my sewing needle rest and listened . . .

"Sometimes I feel like a motherless child . . .
Sometimes I feel like a motherless child . . ."

She knows, I thought, fighting back tears. *She knows how I feel—hot and pregnant and poor—and homesick for Maine* . . . I sucked the row of bloody dots on my finger. I hated patching. I wished I could sew with a thimble.

"Maybe we can," Rev said cheerfully.

"Can what?" Busy feeling sorry for myself, I'd forgotten what I'd said.

"Buy a new record."

"Don't be silly. We'll buy new overalls, if anything. John climbs up and down that pile of old lumber and finds every nail in it—with the seat of his pants."

"All the same—" He stood over me, dark eyes bright with excitement. "I think we'll buy a new Anderson record after my next wedding."

"Wedding?" I perked up instantly. Only heartbreak had been hitting the parish that summer. There'd been no wedding for weeks. We tried to share with our people whatever came, but sharing weddings was fun. Besides, the little envelope was always mine—the one bit of cash a minister's wife ever has—to do with exactly as I pleased. I'd bought new wallpaper for the halls with the last one.

"Whose wedding?"

Rev was smiling. He pointed to the phonograph. We'd been speaking softly. The glorious voice still filled the room.

"Hers," he said. "Marian Anderson's."

I couldn't speak. I worshiped Marian Anderson, and Rev knew it . . .

". . . like a motherless child,
A long way from home, a long way from home."

The song ended. "In the church?" I whispered. That would be perfect—the new church, white altar, wine carpet . . .

Rev shook his head. "Church won't be ready till November, dear. She's being married two weeks from today, here, in the parsonage . . . now what in the world are you crying about? I thought you'd be glad!"

"Glad!" I was on my feet, pointing. "Look at the wallpaper, the sofa! Look at the raggedy old lace curtains, the chairs—all different colors! Look at *everything* in this God-forsaken place—" I wasn't really thinking of God, but Rev, as usual, made me.

" 'God-forsaken' on purpose, dear. You know we agreed to tackle the church first."

"I know—" Church and parsonage had both been falling apart when we'd come there two years before. There'd been serious talk of closing up shop, selling the property to pay old bills. Rev had deliberately encouraged the people to pour every cent into rebuilding their sanctuary. Worship, he'd said, was the most important thing. They'd gone along with him, but this, of course, had meant no money for the parsonage. And in this parsonage nothing could be done without money.

This was no little bungalow, no small Cape Cod that a clever wife could make pretty with a few yards of chintz and some pots of philodendron. This was a four-storyed Victorian monstrosity. Fifteen vast rooms, each twelve feet high, gloomy, dark, and in sad disrepair, opened one into another through ten-foot arches. Nothing could be hidden. Nothing, except possibly the kitchen, could be shut off.

"I know—" I said again, "but if I'd ever dreamed Marian Anderson—"

"She won't be looking at wallpaper," Rev tried to comfort me. "She'll be looking at Mr. Fisher. She's known him for a long time, and they're in love—so much in love they don't want reporters trailing them all during their honeymoon. That's what she's mainly concerned about, dear—keeping her marriage secret for a few weeks, so you're not to tell anyone."

"Of course not," I agreed. "Just Julie." Julie Hibbard was my best friend. She worked for Ruth and Edna Terry in the town's only bookstore, lived two doors down from the parsonage, and was my ever-present help in time of trouble. I never could have lived in that awful house without Julie.

"No," said my husband sternly. "Not even Julie."

"But she's in and out of here every day! She knows everything I do! And she won't tell—"

"Listen to me, dear. Miss Anderson's not even coming to the town hall to get her marriage license. She's going to the town clerk's home at ten o'clock at night so she won't be seen. You're not to tell ***anyone.*** Do you understand?"

"But I can't possibly get this house ready without Julie! She'll help, and she'll never breathe a word—" I was talking fast, but Rev was shaking his head even faster.

"No."

Still I protested. "She'll want to know why all the fuss! She knows I'm three months' pregnant, and still nauseous, and she knows I never—I never—" I stopped. Rev laughed.

"She knows you never clean up unless somebody's coming," he said tolerantly. "Well, somebody is coming—Bishop Francis John McConnell. Remember? Tell Julie you're cleaning up for him."

"In July? For someone coming in November? She'll never believe it. She knows I never do things that far ahead."

"Tell her you're making a real effort this time. No Bishop's been in this church at all for more than fifty years. Tell her you're planning ahead, getting everything done on account of the baby . . . Most ministers' wives would—" he laid it on a little. "It's perfectly natural to fuss for a bishop."

"I suppose so." I was not convinced. November was a long way off. I'd never even met Bishop McConnell. I loved Marian Anderson, and she was coming in two weeks. I needed a friend.

"Remember," Rev said again, going off to make his parish calls, "not even Julie."

I sat down on the worn brown sofa, automatically pushing down the black spring sticking up from the middle cushion, and looked around my house—trying to picture it as the scene of Marian Anderson's wedding, trying to think what I could do by myself to make it right for her, trying to analyze why this seemed so ridiculously impossible.

It was not that Marian Anderson was a celebrity. No Maine girl is ever too impressed by celebrities. Like most University of Maine co-eds, I'd put in my stint on Mount Desert Island, waiting on the rich and famous. Edsel Ford had always jumped up to hold open the swinging door when my tray of lobsters had been particularly heavy. I knew how all the Rockefeller boys liked their morning popovers when they came in from horse-back riding round Jordan Pond. I also knew they usually tipped a quarter. I'd helped Henry Van Dyke count straw votes for Al Smith or Herbert Hoover at his pre-election dinner party and listened to Olga Samanaroff, Leopold Stakowski's divorced wife, tinkle away at the piano at her afternoon teas.

Married to a clergyman in southern Connecticut, there'd been more of the same. Rev would come home from marrying someone like Westbrook Pegler's pretty ward and repeat the jokes Fred Allen had told at the reception, and I'd only half listen. But Marian Anderson was different.

She was, I felt, one of the truly great, with a greatness that came from within herself. My feeling for her was all mixed up with my religion, for it seemed to me she was a deeply spiritual person. Listening to her sing often gave me more strength and courage than listening to a dozen sermons—not Rev's, of course. Other ministers'. I knew her wedding would be sacred to her. The setting had to be beautiful, had to be right. My dreary, neglected, shabby, rundown parsonage was completely wrong.

The Gilbert Brothers, lumber dealers, had built it in the 1890s. Loyal Methodists, they honestly considered the minister the most important person in the community. Therefore, he should have the largest, most imposing house. They had put their whole heart and half their lumber yard into building it for him. There were, for example, twenty-seven doors and windows in the halls alone. I knew. Julie and I had sanded and varnished all twenty-seven of them in the spring before Herbie Hopkins had put on the new wallpaper.

Herbie, also a loyal parishioner, had come for seven weeks after his regular day's work to get that job done. He'd spent two weeks steaming off the old paper—five brown layers of it, way down to the original oatmeal. I was evidently the first preacher's wife to take any off, and I was also the first to want to change the color. For when the church women brought a sample of the new paper, it, too, was brown. Halls, they said, were always brown.

I'd rebelled. "Please, Rev, can't I have my choice? I still have my last wedding envelope, and I'll pay the difference, if color's more expensive. But I don't have to have expensive paper—just anything except brown! The whole house is brown! I've got to have some color, or die!"

I don't know what Rev told the ladies, but they had finally consented—some, I heard later, unwillingly. "No knowing what she'll pick out. Heard they painted the kitchen in New Milford bright red."

So I had boarded the Danbury bus one spring morning and spent a glorious day in the paper stores. I'd found an elegant scroll pattern, marked down because it had been discontinued. There were ten rolls of blue scroll on pink, nineteen rolls of pink scroll on blue. We needed, Herbie had said, twenty double rolls to do the job. Surely nineteen was close enough. Six weeks later when we ran out of paper in the upper hall, I realized Herbie had measured very accurately. Julie and I had painted the last wall with blue Kemtone.

Kemtone, I thought. *It wasn't expensive, and there'd been some left over in the can . . . maybe I could charge a few more gallons at the hardware . . . pay for them with Mr. Fisher's little envelope . . . he was bound to be generous . . . must be very proud to be marrying Marian Anderson* . . . I looked up at the twelve-foot ceilings. *Not alone, though. Not without Julie.*

Once more I pushed the black spring down into the sofa cushion, watched it pop up, then stood and like a sleepwalker opened my front door and headed for the house two doors down, rationalizing every step of the way. *It isn't bad news, like a scandal, or an illegitimate baby, that would hurt somebody if I told . . . it's good news, happy news, and Julie will be as excited as I am . . . why, we can lean over the upstairs bannister together and practically see the whole thing* . . . I made a bargain with myself. If Julie were home, I'd tell her. If she wasn't, I'd come straight back and go it alone.

Julie was home.

"It's a crisis," Julie agreed at once. "A real crisis. She's the greatest contralto in the world. Sibelius says so."

"Everybody says so. She's the greatest *anything* America's produced."

"What in the world are we going to do?" That was Julie. She used the plural *we*. Without question she'd thrown herself into my problem.

"Whatever we do, we'll have to do alone. Rev's all tied up, getting the church finished for the bishop's dedication, and there isn't any money. The ladies are even planning a big summer sale. They usually don't do anything in the hot weather."

"It's too bad," Julie mused, "she can't be married in the hall. Your front room's awful, and the middle one's even worse. Where will Rev marry her, anyway?"

"Let's concentrate on the middle room, Julie. We can see right into that from the upstairs bannister, and we could bank the fireplace with greens or something . . ."

"But she'll have to walk through the front room to get there, and once there she can see right into the dining room. That paper's peeling right off the walls."

"I know. John doesn't help. He pulls off a little more every chance he gets . . . maybe there won't be any left on in two weeks. Julie, I've been thinking—you know that blue wall we painted upstairs . . . there's some left in the can. Do you suppose—"

But Julie was way ahead of me. "Blue in the front room! Peppermint pink in the middle! Pick up the colors from the hall paper! Why not? But it'll take gallons. Is there anything in the budget?"

"Just for cloth, not paint. Melissa and Edith have promised to slipcover the old chairs before the Bishop comes . . . but maybe I could charge the paint, pay for it with the little envel—"

"Of course! What are we waiting for?" Julie jumped up and started for the door. "Come on!"

"Permission. That's what we're waiting for. Can't paint anything in a parsonage without permission. Found that out in our first church. Used a little red around the kitchen and they almost made me a member of the New Milford Volunteer Fire Department—"

"Then let's get permission. Come on! I'll ask Rev—"

"Julie, stop!" Suddenly I came out of my sleepwalk, realized what I'd done—disobeyed Rev's request . . . no, disobeyed his direct order . . . deliberately told a parsonage secret . . . Marian Anderson's secret . . . "Julie, you mustn't say a word to Rev. He practically ordered me not to tell anyone about this wedding—even you. Said to let you think I was getting ready for the Bishop—"

"In July? When he's coming in November?" Julie laughed, as I'd known she would. "I know you better than that, my darlin'! But I won't let on. Go alone. Get permission. Get the paint and get brushes—wide ones, the wider the better. We'll start tonight. I'll drop over, real casual-like, the instant the ***Booklet*** closes."

Julie pushed me out into the boiling July sun. Suddenly I thought of those twelve-foot ceilings, step ladders, the smell of Kemtone—I turned back and ran for Julie's sink. With me, morning sickness lasted all day. Julie just handed me a towel and a soda cracker.

"Do—do you think we're tackling too much?" I asked my friend.

"We've only got fourteen—no, thirteen days, and I—I don't feel too peppy. It would look terrible if we got it only half painted."

"It won't be half painted. It'll be whole painted. That stuff goes on fast."

"You—you really think we can do it?"

"Of course we can," said my friend stoutly. "It's for Marian Anderson. Two weeks from today at two o'clock in the afternoon—" Julie spoke solemnly, almost as if she were saying a wedding vow herself—"your whole house—well, at least the downstairs—will be perfectly beautiful."

Julie was right. Two weeks from that moment my drab old parsonage had, indeed, been transformed and was almost, if not perfectly, beautiful, only Marian Anderson never—

To this day my New England conscience bothers me. Would things have turned out differently if I had been a good little parsonage wife, had not disobeyed—not tried to deceive—my husband?

'Bishop and baby both coming . . .'

Two days later Julie and Rev had the blue living room almost painted. I'd taken down the nine pairs of ancient lace curtains, washed them, and was busily darning the fresh crop of holes. I was trying to make my darns look like lace, but not succeeding, when I suddenly remembered the Bleachery and Dye Works in our first parish.

"The Bleachery!" I shouted up to Rev on the ladder. "Why didn't I think of them before? They'd give me cloth, I'm sure! Remember all that shirting they gave us? We sewed surplices for the whole junior choir!"

"Where do you get that *we* stuff?" Rev, watering his can of Kemtone with sweat, was not enthusiastic. Granted we couldn't go to Maine because of the gas rationing, but did we have to spend our whole July vacation slopping paint? He'd even had trouble getting permission. "Paper's only been on those rooms eight years. Perfectly good for another three or four!" But bishops didn't come very often, and when they learned we were buying the paint and putting it on ourselves, permission was granted. So Rev was painting. But that was enough. He had no concept of the master plan Julie and I were ambitiously evolving day by day, and I was carefully mentioning only one thing at a time.

"I asked the man for the cloth," I said, "even if I didn't do much sewing. I'm sure he'd remember me."

"I'm sure he would, too, since you asked for eighty yards. But they only help local churches—do you think they pass out cloth to the whole State of Connecticut?"

"I could say it's for a special occasion, very special." I'd stopped darning holes.

"I heard," Rev discouraged me, "they're under government contract now. Only dyeing for the Army. You don't want khaki curtains."

"Drapes, not curtains. Lovely deep blue drapes. ***I*** heard they're dyeing for the Navy." I wadded up the old lace curtain and wiped up the last blob of paint Rev had let drop. "You're wasting paint."

He peered down from the ladder. "And you're counting chickens. Those old curtains'll never stand being scrubbed with turpentine."

"They never will be. I've got faith. Marian Anderson does a lot for the Lord. I'm sure He wants her to have a nice wedding . . . May I have the car tomorrow, dear? This is certainly 'parish business.'"

"'Parsonage business,'" Rev corrected.

"But you never use all your gas ration, and I'll take John with me. You can have a long, quiet morning to work on your sermon."

"Thanks . . . let's see—I preach again in about four weeks, the first Sunday in August. This is vacation, remember?"

"Please, Rev—it's only twenty miles."

"Oh, all right. Go if you like. But don't be disappointed if they turn you down."

I leaned over once more and wiped up the latest blob with the darned old lace curtain. I was sure they would not turn me down.

Mr. Tetro remembered me, and he was very kind. Yes, he'd heard we'd moved. Where to? Well, now, that wasn't so very far, was it. New drapes I needed? For a special occasion? Well, now, guessed they could spare a few yards—how many? Whew! New parsonage must have a lot of windows! Sure I'd measured right? Hundred-and-seventeen yards was a lot of cloth! Blue be O.K.? Dyeing for the Marines this week. Some had come through with a little white streak up and down the selvage. Was I gonna turn a hem? Well, then, prob'ly wouldn't show a mite. He'd bring a few bolts and see if I liked the color . . .

What color is lovelier than Marine blue? I taught John the words, and we sang at the top of our voices all the way home—

> *"From the halls of Mon-te-zu-ma*
> *to the shores of Tri-po-li—*
> *we will fight our country's ba-a-tles*
> *on the land and on the sea—"*

And on Saipan, I thought, remembering Corporal William D. Shaw, Jr. Bill had been wearing dress blues the day he'd come to say goodbye, before Saipan . . . Yes, I'd be proud to dress my living room in Marine blue, with or without a white streak down the selvage.

That's probably why I decided to hem them by hand. Julie helped me measure and cut out, and I stitched the tops, putting in buckram pinch pleats, but the sides and bottoms were going to be hand-hemmed.

Each of the nine drapes was three yards long, and each window had two drapes. Six times nine is fifty-four, but every drape has two sides and a bottom, so multiply by two and add eighteen—one-hundred-and-twenty-six yards. This was a long way to go by hand—let's see, multiply by twelve, one-thousand-five-hundred-and-twelve feet—especially by a hand that had never learned to sew with a thimble. The white streak near the selvage did, indeed, disappear in the hem, as Mr. Tetro had said, but little dots of dark red blood along the way did not.

"You're a fool." Rev was carefully painting around the fireplace tiles in the pink living room. "You'll never get them done. Put them on the machine and get it over with."

"I still have nine days, and nine nights, too. So glad to get rid of those old lace things, I'd hold the needle in my teeth if that would make a better edge."

"The way you sew, would it make any difference?" I forgave him. I knew he thought I was making altogether too much fuss about a certain parsonage wedding, but Julie had just left, suggesting cornice boards out of the old lumber in the backyard and he'd agreed to nail some boards together. For nine pink and blue cornices, I'd have forgiven much more. For my sewing was slow. I still had seven windows to go two nights later when Julie waylaid Melissa and Edith after choir rehearsal.

These sisters slipcovered and draped all the well-to-do houses for miles around. They were professionals, but, reared in Methodist parsonages, they honored their reverend father's memory by always taking a lively interest in the one nearest them. Lucky for me, this was mine.

"Getting ready for the Bishop?" Melissa, the plump one, bustled in.

"Not going to Maine for your vacation?" Edith, the slim one, was right behind her. I said 'yes' and Rev said 'no' but neither sister paid much attention. They were both examining the edge of my drape.

"Glad you're hand-hemming," Edith approved.

"Can't stand machine-stitched drapes," Melissa agreed. Rev glared at both of them.

"Do you like the pink and blue paint?" I asked anxiously. These two were the decorating arbiters of the parish. If they approved the paint, no one else would disapprove—at least, not out loud.

"Blue's a lovely shade," said Edith.

"So's the pink," said Melissa.

"Praise the Lord!" I said silently.

"Painting's hard work in this heat." Julie, wielding the second brush, tossed in her two cents' worth. "But it's going to be such a busy fall—"

"Bishop coming—" interrupted Melissa.

"Baby coming—" Edith said at the same time.

"Bishop and baby both coming . . ." I said.

"And you never can tell about babies . . ." Julie speculated. Both sisters eyed me with their mental tape-measure. I stuck out my stomach and tried to look as pregnant and pathetic as possible. I didn't have to try very hard. I'd been sewing all day.

"Bishop and baby both," I said plaintively. Both sisters played the organ and recognized the tremulo stop. "I don't suppose you girls would want to start the slip covers—"

"Sofa's certainly shabby." Edith pushed down the black spring.

"Especially against the new paint." The spring popped up again. Melissa pushed down—harder. But still the spring popped up.

"Shabby's right!" Julie pulled out a stop or two herself. "Why, Mother's got an old sofa out in our barn looks better'n this one. Been trying to find someone to cart it to the dump. Have you finished with Rachel?"

"Delivered tonight," said Melissa.

"All but the night gowns," Edith amended. "She's fussy about her night gowns. Wears 'em to write in. I made the one for ***Susan and God,***" she added proudly. Julie winked at me behind Rev's back. Rachel Crothers was small potatoes compared to Marian Anderson.

"Must be wonderful," Julie said, "to sew for famous people like that . . . make their night gowns and all. ***John McLean's*** is having a fabric sale."

"Cloth in the budget?" Edith wanted to know.

"Money in the budget?" Melissa was more specific.

"Yes," chorused three voices. Rev from the fireplace, I on the floor, and even Julie on the ladder all spoke at once. Julie was a devout Episcopalian, but always knew what was available for the Methodist parsonage. Cloth had been budgeted, and there was money.

"Stripes would be smart." Melissa eyed the sofa. "A pink stripe, with a fine red line, for the sofa in the blue room—"

Edith picked up the theme dreamily. "And a blue stripe, for the sofa in the pink room—" I looked around both rooms. Had I missed something?

"But girls—there's only one sofa!"

"Didn't you say, dear," Edith said to Julie, "that your mother has an old sofa out in her barn?"

"Just waiting," Melissa headed for the door, "to be carted to the dump?"

"Goodnight, all!" Edith called back.

The next morning George Britto brought the sofa, still smelling slightly of timothy, from Julie's barn, and the sisters bought their pink and blue stripes at ***John McLean's.*** They also bought plain pink or blue fabric for the half-dozen assorted chairs. I still had six windows to go when they stopped by to cut out the covers. I was having difficulty threading my needle when they came, and I'd just about threaded it and tied the knot when they left.

"Take 'em home. Stitch 'em up," Melissa said cheerfully.

"Bring 'em back in a day or so." Edith waved goodbye.

I was dumbfounded. "Did you see that?" I asked Rev, busy nailing up a cornice. "Is that all there is to slip-covering? Toss the cloth over the chair, make a swipe or two with a piece of chalk, whack away with the shears for a minute, take 'em home and stitch 'em up? Why, I could've—"

"Don't you try it," he warned, "ever. And by the way, is there going to be any dinner? Pulling nails out of old lumber gives a man an appetite, especially when his wife forgot about lunch."

Rev headed for the back yard to find boards for another cornice. I put down my drape, called John to come with me, and headed for the First National. Meat was rationed, of course, and scarce. Standing in the meat line from seven in the morning till the store opened took altogether too much time. We'd been living on scrambled eggs and cheese sandwiches. But I'd better feed him—

The composer's wife contributes . . .

Mrs. Charles Ives was coming out of the store and stopped to pat John's head. Her husband, who was to win a Pulitzer for his music, spent his weekends composing. One seldom saw him. But Mrs. Ives was in her pew in Rev's Long Ridge church every Sunday. There was a bit of rivalry between the two parishes for the minister's time and attention. Right now Hilda Ives, who adored Rev, thought Bethel was getting more than its share. She was worried about him.

"He's been working so hard on that church, and now I hear he's spending his whole vacation painting the parsonage! That's ridiculous. Can't they afford to hire a painter?"

"Not a chance," I told her. "Too many expensive things to buy before the dedication. The ladies are even planning a summer sale."

Mrs. Ives went down the street, shaking her head. She believed in stewardship, not in sales. A moment later she was back, pushing something into my hand.

"Use it in the parsonage, dear—any way you like. You look tired, too." She was gone before I could say thank-you. I unrolled a twenty-dollar bill.

How good people are! I marveled. *And how wonderful—the wife of a great American composer helps me get my house ready for the wedding of a great American singer! Wish I could tell her! . . . 'any way you like,' she said . . .*

I knew exactly what way I liked. The Danbury bus was slowing down outside the First National. I grabbed John's hand. If we hurried—it really wouldn't hurt Rev to eat scrambled eggs one more night. We climbed aboard.

An hour later we climbed down again, John carrying one roll and I nine rolls of blue scroll on pink. It had still been there, unsold and marked down even more since spring. With the rest of the twenty dollars, I could pay Herbie for putting it on. I called him while I stirred the scrambled eggs, told him this was a paid job, and he was there before we'd finished eating. With John happily doing the lion's share, we ripped off what was left of ugly brown, and Herbie started slapping on sky blue. Paid jobs go much faster than unpaid. Two days later the dining room was freshly papered, with a whole roll left over.

Julie was delirious. "Didn't I tell you?" she bubbled whenever Rev's back was turned. "I ***knew*** we could do it! Can't you hurry with those drapes? How many more windows?"

"Only three. And I wish you wouldn't get so excited, Julie. Rev's smart, you know."

"I haven't said a word!" Julie wiped her fingers. She'd cut twenty-seven scrolls from the left-over paper and pasted three on each cornice. "Aren't the scrolls beautiful? Maybe I should've been a decorator."

"A decorator maybe, but not an actress. I saw Rev looking at you several times last night—you were humming ***Motherless Child.***"

"***Anyone*** can hum a spiritual!" She ran cold water into the paste pan. "But I was going to take a little walk tonight anyway—going over to see how the slip covers are coming along."

Julie went off, humming ***Swing Low, Sweet Chariot*** under her breath. She'd come early and stayed late for nearly two weeks now. I loved her, but I also loved my husband, and he had given an explicit order concerning my friend Julie . . .

She was back a half-hour later, carrying two bulging shopping bags.

"What's that?"

"Scraps! Pink and blue, from all the covers! Guess what—I'm going to braid a rug for her to stand on!"

"Do you know how?"

"Sure, learned how way back in Brownies. Had a craft leader once that couldn't do anything else. Spent one whole winter braiding rugs." Julie grabbed the yard stick and knelt down before the fireplace. "You're sure this is where Rev'll marry her?"

"It's ***them,*** Julie, not ***her.*** Mr. Orpheus Fisher, nickname 'King.' Takes two to get married, you know. Your rug can't be too little."

"Mmm—sure hope I've got enough scraps—and that ***this*** Kingfisher has small feet—"

"How are the slip covers coming?"

Julie looked at my drape. I was plodding wearily on, leaving my trail of bloody dots.

"They'll be done before you are. Edith was tying down that black spring in the sofa cushion—going to miss that old pop-up—they'll bring 'em over soon, they said."

Julie was right. I still had one whole window to go—fourteen yards of hemming—the day before the wedding when the sisters came in laden with covers. They'd heard about the dining room paper and were eager to see it.

"Why, it's like the hall!" Melissa craned her neck.

"Only opposite!" Edith craned, too.

"Is that bad?" I asked worriedly, "To have the same pattern?" I'd hopped on that Danbury bus so fast that day I'd completely forgotten to ask permission.

"Not bad at all," said Edith

"Better that way," Melissa agreed, "especially with the stripes." I drew a deep breath. *Praise the Lord!* I said—under it.

The sisters tossed new covers over the two sofas, over the motley chairs, tucked in the folds with their yard stick, gave a tug here and a poke there—and it was like a miracle! Every cover fitted perfectly. I looked at my bloody middle finger and made up my mind then and there to learn to sew with a thimble. There was an immense difference, I could plainly see, between professional and amateur.

Edith stood back, surveying the pink sofa. "There!"

Melissa smiled, smoothing the blue. "Done!"

"You should feel proud!" I praised them both. "***W & J Sloane*** never did any better!"

Julie agreed. "They're beautiful! Are there any more scraps?" Her oval rug was only two feet long. She still had no idea how long Mr. Fisher's feet were.

"Some in the car," said Edith.

"Don't waste much cloth," said Melissa.

"You don't waste any!" I went from chair to chair, admiring their work. "Sit down, girls. You should be the first to sit on them! I'll make lemonade."

We were still admiring the new covers and drinking lemonade when the phone rang. It was Zula Trimpert, the doctor's wife, two doors up, and she didn't sound like herself. The Trimperts' son, Eugene, was the same age as John. They played together constantly, and Zula often didn't sound like herself when she called me. This time she came right to the point.

"Do you know," she asked icily, "where your son is?"

"Of course," I answered righteously—and placatingly. "He and

Genie are playing on the front porch—heard their voices just a moment ago. Genie looks so cute in his white sailor suit—can't you come over a minute, Zu, before you leave? See my new slip covers? The girls just brought them, and we're all sitting here admiring—"

"Eugene's ***not*** on your front porch," she interrupted. "He's in my bathtub, and he's not white. He's pink and blue all over. Perhaps you should forget your slip-covers for a minute and go tend your child." Zula was a real Southern lady and would never in the world bang a telephone receiver. But it did go down hard.

"Odd—" I told the girls. "Zu says Genie's pink and blue all over."

"Must mean black and blue," Melissa, married but childless, smiled comfortably.

"Probably took a little tumble," Edith, unmarried, smiled too. But Julie, who knew John rather well, had headed for the front porch.

"Come quick!" she called. I also knew John. I ran.

My son, too, was pink and blue all over, and so was our thirty-foot porch. Bright pink and blue stripes, like a carousel awning, went up and down the clapboards, as high as two-year-old arms could reach. John gave me an angelic, pink-and-blue smile.

"Fixin' up," he said, "for the Bishop. Don't worry 'bout the outside, Mommy. Genie 'n me'll do it—only he quit," he added scornfully. "Paint in his eye."

"Look out!" Julie was aiming the garden hose. "Have to hose the house quick, before it dries!"

"Hose the boy, too—" I covered the Kemtone cans I'd foolishly left on the porch and pried the big brush from the small fist. "Can't paint the outside just yet, son. It's too big a job, and there isn't enough paint. Wait till you're three—then we'll tackle it."

'Use Scotch tape and come to bed!'

Zula was right, of course. I had been neglecting the child for the house. The last thirteen days John had had the longest play baths and the shortest stories of his life. That night after supper I lay down on his bed and read ***The Little Engine That Could*** three times, as requested, and sang ***Sometimes I Feel like a Motherless Child*** until he fell asleep. Then I kissed the still faintly blue head and went downstairs to my drape. Twelve yards to go.

"No wonder he tried to get in on the act," I told Julie. "Everyone else is . . . I'm really proud of him, wanting to help."

Julie was pressing her rug with a wet towel, trying to stretch it a bit bigger. "Good thing it was water paint. Oil would've been the dickens to get off."

"Off house, or off boy?"

"Off Genie and his white sailor suit. Never saw Zu so angry. She had him all dressed up—they were going to stop for dinner on the way to Boston. Kept Doc waiting an hour while she scrubbed . . . I didn't dare ask her for flowers."

"But we have to have flowers!" Most people's gardens had died down by the last of July, especially Julie's and my unwatered ones, but Zu, Southern-bred, knew how to keep hers blossoming through the hottest summer. We'd counted on her flowers. All I had in bloom were a few tomato plants.

"Well, I did mention that I'd keep them cut for her till they get back—you know, so they won't go to seed." Julie was grinning.

"Well, flowers go to seed awfully fast this hot weather. You'd better get right over there—tonight."

"Brought a flashlight. Just want to finish my rug first. Do you ***really*** think they'll stand on it?"

"Put it right there and you can't miss."

"I'll keep it forever, if they do." Julie was on her hands and knees by the fireplace, still stretching. "Just not sure it's big enough for four feet."

"Then put it a little to the left. You know—bride always stands on the left." Julie carefully placed the pink-and-blue rug off-center and, flashlight in hand, went off. I was on the floor, keeping doggedly on with my drape, when I heard Rev come in the back door, start opening cupboards.

"What's this cake?" he called. "Home or church?"

"The frosted one? Don't touch it! You know the sale's tomorrow. Yours is in the breadbox."

He strolled in, glass of milk in one hand, huge wedge of scorched, unfrosted chocolate cake in the other.

"Make this one first?"

"Yes . . . why?"

"Just wondered. Suppose if you hadn't burned it, John and I'd be out of luck altogether."

"Food—" I said scornfully. "Don't bother me. I'm an interior decorator."

"Mmm—so I noticed. Any chance of decorating me a little, like with a clean shirt? Don't suppose she'll be looking at anything but the drapes, but maybe I should put on a clean shirt, just in case—"

I pointed to the hall. "There are six clean, ironed shirts right there in that basket."

"Six! Can't believe it . . . been wearing them hot from the iron lately." He went to look. "Mmm—folded . . . you always put 'em on hangers. Mother Thurner's an old lady, dear. You really shouldn't let her do your ironing."

"***Let*** her! I didn't ***let*** her! Didn't even know she was doing it. She just pulled the shirts off the line, took them home, and brought them back ironed."

"Washed, too, by the looks. Noticed they were kind of speckled when I mowed the lawn, er—day before yesterday. How old would you say Mother Thurner is, dear? About seventy-five?"

"I tell you I never missed the old shirts! And you're supposed to leave clothes out in the sun—to—to bleach them. And besides, you told me yourself I was too independent! Said I should learn to accept, and receive, and—and give people an opportunity to show love—"

Rev threw back his head and roared. "That must have been before we were married, darlin'! You've had both parishes waiting on you—hand, foot, and finger—for five years now! Especially this one—the last two weeks. Let's see—" He counted on his fingers. "Mother Thurner, and Herbie Hopkins, and Melissa and Edith, and money from Hilda Ives, and cloth from Fred Tetro, and, of course, our friend Julie—" He stopped, looked around. "Where is our little helper tonight? Don't tell me she's gone home early!"

"She—she's coming back. She's out picking flowers."

"At ten-thirty? In the dark?"

"She—she has a flashlight. She's keeping Zu's flowers cut, while they're on vacation, so—so they won't go to seed."

Rev looked at his watch. "Let's see—Trimp pulled out around half-past five. Been gone five hours. Julie better hurry. Won't be a flower left by morning. Just seeds."

I was hemming fast—and crooked. Every time he needled me, I needled myself. The dots were getting bigger and redder.

"She's cutting pink cosmos and red zinnias, if you want to know. We both wanted to see how they'll look against the blue wall."

"Tonight?" Rev persisted. "Julie wanted to see how they'd look tonight?" I knew what he meant—the night before Marian Anderson's wedding. He'd known for days that I'd told Julie our secret, but he was going to make me say it.

"She—she's picking hydrangeas, too—lots of them, pink and blue, and—and breaking off pine branches. We're going to bank the fireplace and—and fill every vase."

I didn't look up, but it was confession, and he recognized it as such. I felt better already. Now if he'd only forgive me, maybe I could take a deep breath and ***really*** enjoy Marian Anderson's wedding.

"Thought Julie was pushing too hard—just a bit too hard, in July, for a bishop in November. Going to lean over the upstairs bannister? It's shaky, you know . . . how many've you invited—Melissa? Edith?—"

"Of course not!" I was indignant. "I haven't told a soul but Julie, and she hasn't breathed it!"

"Maybe she hasn't breathed it, but she's been singing spirituals—off-key, by the way—for a week. She make this thing for them to stand on?" He centered the braided rug with his toe.

"Yes, she did—I'm sorry, Rev. It—it was just too much for me alone . . . but I've felt miserable ever since—" More drops fell on the drape. Not blood, this time. He knelt down on Julie's rug, put his hand under my chin.

"Look at me . . . it means so much to you, the looks of this old place, for a ten-minute wedding?"

I nodded. "Don't you see? It's the greatest moment of her life. It always is, for every woman, and I know it'll be for her, because she feels things . . . Rev, she's sung all over the world, for kings and queens, but the greatest moment of her life will be right here, in our home . . . it ***has*** to be right for her—" He kissed my wet cheeks, held his handkerchief under my nose.

"Blow."

I knew by the tone I was forgiven. I also knew it wasn't worth it. I was through deceiving my husband. "Can't you come to bed?" he whispered. "Now? You've worked late every night . . . and been up early every morning—"

"Got some beauties!" Julie called from the kitchen. "Cosmos, zinnias, the works!" She stood in the arch, her arms filled with blossoms. "Oh, hi, Rev. You home?"

He stood up. "I do drop in—occasionally. Not that it makes much difference. Good night, girls—" He started upstairs. "Be here well before two o'clock tomorrow, Julie. And don't lean too hard on the bannister. You might drop in on the ceremony unexpectedly." He stopped, leaned far over the bannister himself.

"And as for those damn drapes," he shouted down, "I'm sick of 'em! Use Scotch tape and come to bed!" The bedroom door slammed.

Julie was thunderstruck. She'd never heard Rev swear before.

"He knows you told me! How in the world did he find out?"

"He's known for days, Julie." I was rummaging in my desk. "He always knows things like that—he's a minister."

"Don't know if I'd like being married to a man who knows everything—"

"It's not so bad . . . help me spread this drape, dear—and he's not really angry—just worried 'cause we've been working so hard—"

We laid the last drape flat on the floor and did in two minutes with Scotch tape what would have taken two hours by hand.

"Why in the world didn't we think of this before! You cover books, and I used to teach school! No stitches and no dots on the front, either! It's better than thread!"

Julie climbed the ladder, fastened drapery hooks under the ninth cornice.

"Not washable, though. Better hem it before the Bishop comes. Shall I start arranging?" She climbed down.

"Do you mind, Julie, if we put the flowers in water tonight?" I was snapping off lights. "I'm sort of tired—really want to go to bed—"

Julie didn't mind. She trudged cheerfully off toward home. I crept up the stairs and quietly opened the bedroom door. John wasn't the only boy in my family I'd been neglecting lately. Rev doesn't say ***Damn*** very often.

Fully forgiven the next morning and feeling better than I had for days, I taught John to sing ***Here Comes the Bride*** as we filled my wedding vases with pink cosmos, red zinnias, banked the fireplace with fragrant pine. Flowers were the final touch. The rooms came alive.

"Everything pretty." John disappeared for a few minutes, came back with his sand pail filled with witchgrass and my few tomato blossoms. "All fixed up," he said, "for the Bishop."

"Yes," I said. "He'll be along, a little later." Hand in hand we walked through each room, admiring the flowers, the blue drapes, the scrolls on the cornice boards, the striped sofas. "The rooms are saying 'thank you,' " I told my son. "They like being fussed over, the same as people."

"Want me to preach you a sermon?" he asked gravely. I glanced at my watch. An hour until the sale started, and everything was ready.

"Certainly, son." I sat in a pink chair and reached for the Bible. John climbed onto a blue one, stood in the seat, leaning against the back. I didn't reprimand him. This as a 'Daddy' game we often played. Slipcovers are washable, and a boy has to have a pulpit.

"First hymn. "*From the halls of Mon-te-zu-ma to the shores of Trip-o-li* . . ." We sang it together.

"Every day, every day, for you the spirit of God is here . . . I'm sure, I'm sure, I'm sure so. Bible now, Mommy. House on the rocks."

"Very appropriate scripture," I told him, turning to Matthew's 7th chapter. '*. . . and the rain descended, and the floods came, and the winds blew, and beat upon that house, and it fell not, for it was founded upon a rock—*' "

"Nuff! Sermon now. Seas bang up against the rocks. Seas against the ground. It never gets drowned. You know the house on the rock? For you the love of God comes down, every day, every day, I'm sure so. Down comes God with a bundle of love . . . down, down, down. There's teenie-weenies down there, and funny pies. You know who funny pies are? They're devils. I'm not fooling. It's written in the book . . . Amen."

"Fine sermon, son." I was searching my pockets.

"Off'ring now." John hopped down and held out his hand. This, too, was part of the game. I put in a dime.

"Shall we use this offering to feed the hungry?"

"I'm hungry," said John.

"Well, then, let's go next door. They're selling cookies over there." We took the frosted cake, securely fastened with toothpicks, from the pantry and walked across the drive to the summer sale. Clothesline cord was strung from maple to maple, dozens of aprons fluttering from it. I went behind the food table, put down my cake, and sold John his cookies. Other women were coming with pies, more cakes, and homemade bread. Townspeople were lining up to buy, for everyone knows the best stuff goes first.

I sold food for an hour or so and then shifted to the less-busy plant table. By now the church lawns were jammed with people. Baby pictures of town officials—lying on their belly on bearskin rugs—had been tacked up as a guessing game, and everyone clapped when Mother Thurner identified the fattest baby as Morey Britto, the town's only policeman.

Suddenly I remembered another church lawn, another crowd clapping, clapping, a bride and groom running toward a car . . . There'd been an auction next door to the church the day Rev and I'd been married. *But Marian Anderson doesn't want clapping,* I thought. *She doesn't even want to be seen*—And then I heard the parsonage phone.

A wisp of white veiling

Rev was talking as I rushed in. "Yes, yes . . . it goes on most of the day, or at least till everything's sold . . . No, of course you don't . . . I understand. I'll do my best to find a place . . . I'm sorry." He glanced at me. "My—my wife is going to be very disappointed . . . Yes, I'll call you."

I sat down on the blue-striped sofa. "You're not going to marry her."

"Of course I'm going to marry her, dear—only not here. She's upset. They drove by and saw the crowd." He was leafing through the phone book. "Have to find another place—somewhere private. Why didn't we think about the sale?"

"Too busy thinking about the house . . . do you remember our wedding, Rev? All the people clap—"

"What's that trustee's name . . . here it is—King . . . Said she's wearing a long gown, white satin . . . Of course she'd be noticed coming in, dressed like that."

"She wouldn't wear anything else . . . I kept telling you—her wedding's important. Who's Mr. King?"

"Trustee of Elmwood Chapel. Remember it? Brown shingles? About five miles out? . . . Hello, Mr. King? This is Jack Grenfell here in Bethel . . ."

He talked to the trustee about the use of Elmwood Chapel for a little wedding—oh, no, nothing suspicious . . . couple just wanted to keep their marriage quiet for awhile . . ."

I looked around the empty rooms. "All fixed up," John had said, "for the Bishop." I hoped he'd be coming. No one else was . . .

Mr. King lived in Danbury, seven miles away. It was well past noon when Rev got back with the key. The Chapel was five miles in the opposite direction.

"Better come with me," he called from the door. "King says the place hasn't been used since Children's Day. Might have to clean it." I climbed into the car. *Two weeks,* I thought. *Two weeks working night and day to fix up one shabby old place, and here we are, racing over the roads to fix up another one—in fifteen minutes.*

Cobwebs brushed our faces as we walked in. Last June's dead daisies still wreathed the posts, the altar rail. Dried roses, stiff and brittle, stood in waterless vases.

"Wish I'd thought to bring some flowers—and Julie's rug . . . could at least have done that."

"You've done enough. See a broom anywhere?" Rev was rummaging in closets. He started for the door. "Have to borrow one from the neighbors."

"Not across the street," I warned. "Remember who lives there?"

"Holy Smoke! Forgot all about her!" Rev headed down the road. I started pulling off dead daisies.

Gladys Merrill, town reporter for the ***Bridgeport Post,*** lived across from Elmwood Chapel. Where news was concerned, Gladys had the nose of a beagle and the eyes of a hawk. Our church wasn't being dedicated till November, but she'd already interviewed Rev twice, read a life of John Wesley, and memorized all Francis John's degrees from ***Who's Who***.

It was hard to keep anything from Gladys, and now Rev had arranged what would undoubtedly be the scoop of her life right under her nose. We'd have to think of something. Couldn't keep Marian Anderson chasing around the Connecticut countryside all afternoon in white satin looking for a place to be married that didn't have church sales or newpaper reporters . . .

Rev came back. Made the dirt fly. My search for a dust cloth was as futile as his for a broom. I pulled off my maternity slip and set to work. It was expendable. We'd given so much . . . what was one more white petticoat with a round hole in the front?

"No more time . . . have to dress." He drove even faster on the way home, but it was one-thirty when we hurried up the parsonage steps.

"My, you folks are busy today," one of the ladies called.

"Does that mean I should still be over there, selling cookies?" I followed Rev upstairs.

"Don't be silly. Empty my brief case," he called from the shower. "Pack my robe in it—and the ***Ritual*** and certificate on the mantel downstairs . . . and watch for her car. It won't turn in, just slow down . . . No, I ***don't*** want a glass of milk! . . . and be sure to call Gladys . . ."

That was the plan we'd worked out. I was to call our reporter friend and keep her on the phone as long as it would take Marian Anderson to go into the Chapel, be married, come out, and drive away.

Rev ran down the stairs, struggling with his back stud. "Call her about eight minutes after I leave, dear, and keep her talking—"

"How long?"

"Well—till I get back!"

"Fine." My heart wasn't in it. I picked a pink thread off his black trouser leg. "What'll I tell her?"

"Don't tell her anything! That's why you're calling her! You're sure her phone's in the back of the house?"

"Positive. In her kitchen. And she has only one—Gladys is economical."

"Good—" Rev was standing just inside the screen door. Two o'clock. I came and stood beside him. Maybe I'd see her face—

"I'm sorry, darlin'," he whispered. "All your work—wish you could come, too." I didn't answer. What was there to say? "Where's John?"

"Having lunch at Julie's—probably napping. I told her, while you were getting the keys . . . Is that the car?"

A black sedan slowed down in front of the parsonage. Rev ran down the steps, opened the car door. I caught a glimpse of dark hair, the gleam of satin, a wisp of white veiling . . . the car was gone. On the church lawn the ladies were busily marking down the last of their wares to bargain prices. I locked the front door, looked at my watch, went to sit by the phone . . .

What could I say to Gladys? More about Rev—how he'd almost drowned playing in pirate caves in Cornwall? been soloist on a Boston radio station when he was in college? drama coach for five years at a YMCA camp? . . . Maybe more about the Bethel church—did she know someone had given beautiful new brass for the altar? and that Walter Tittle, who'd designed the new steeple, was in Washington painting Roosevelt for the fourth time? . . . More about Francis John—did she know he'd just mediated a steel strike, that labor really trusted him? . . . and if I ran out of grown-ups, I could always talk about boys. Gladys had one of her own named Terry, the same age as John and even messier . . .

One more minute . . . I looked at Julie's little rug. It was about to happen—this moment we'd prepared for so lovingly—only not here, not here at all . . . somewhere else . . .

Gladys's phone rang and rang. Where was she? Investigating the open windows in the Chapel? Snapping a picture of Marian Anderson? Asking Rev—"Gladys! Hi! Thought you weren't home! . . . Oh, weeding your front borders? Well, sit down a minute. I want to tell you about—"

I was still telling her forty minutes later—Gladys didn't call ***me*** again till November!—when Rev unlocked the front door. "Bye, Gladys. Keep in touch."

I put down the phone. My arm ached. My ear ached. And there was another kind of dull ache somewhere inside. Marian Anderson's wedding was over. Rev put his hand on my shoulder.

"Good job, darling. Did you keep her talking all this time?"

"Had to . . . she's weeding her front borders this afternoon, right alongside the road. They'd have honeymooned with every reporter on the ***Bridgeport Post*** if I'd ever hung up. How was it?"

"The way she wanted it, I think—simple, and sincere, and sacred . . ."

"She didn't mind the place? . . . half clean? . . . no flowers?"

"Her bouquet was beautiful, dear, and I've been trying to tell you—marriage doesn't have much to do with—with paint or wallpaper or slipcovers. It's an inside thing. She said the Chapel reminded her of the little church where she started Sunday School."

I looked around at the big rooms. Suddenly they looked theatrical, like a giant stage set—delicate pink, sky blue, certainly impractical for a home with two children—even a little gaudy. I started to cry.

"I've been a fool, Rev, a complete fool. But never again. I ***know*** marriage is an inside thing . . . why wouldn't I, married to you . . . I'm glad she liked the little chapel—"

Rev pulled the linen handkerchief from his breast pocket. "It's all right, honey . . . want your little envelope?" He took that, too, out of his pocket.

"I—I don't really care, except for the paint. Have to pay for that." I opened the envelope. "It'll just about do it—"

"The ladies are paying for the paint, dear, with the sale money. They're really proud of what you've done, getting the parsonage all ready for the Bishop, and so far ahead . . ." He grinned, pulled me to my feet. "We were going to do something else with this envelope—remember? Let's get our friend Julie and our son John and go pick out our new Marian Anderson record."

I glanced back at the ninth window. "Have to hem that last drape," I said, "sometime . . . ."

DEDICATION SUNDAY AT THE NEWLY BUILT BETHEL METHODIST CHURCH, NOVEMBER, 1943. Inside the chancel are (l. to r.) Church School Superintendent Frank Berry, who was also superintendent of Bethel Public Schools; the Reverend Jack Grenfell, Pastor; Dr. Norman Twiddy, District Superintendent of Methodist churches in Southern Connecticut; and the Reverend Dr. Francis John McConnell, dearly loved Bishop of the New York East Conference of the Methodist Church.

'. . . unfailing courage, hard work, determined faith . . .'

I fully meant to. Where did the months go? Miss Anderson enjoyed her secret honeymoon, I washed John's old baby clothes, hopefully changing blue ribbons to pink, Rev worked hard to finish the church, and then—a Friday night of hectic phone calls—***NEW YORK CALLING . . . BOSTON CALLING . . . Is Miss Anderson married? . . . Did she wear white satin?***—a Saturday of hammering carpet tacks and reading newspapers, and suddenly it was Sunday morning and John and I were sitting with ***The Order for the Dedication of a Church*** in our hands, listening to Francis John. We could barely see him above the baskets of flowers.

It seemed as if everyone of every faith who had worked on the church for the past two years had sent flowers. Bernie Dolan of Dolan Construction Company, the best Roman Catholic friend a Methodist church ever had, who, before Rev came, had carried the coal bill unpaid for five years; Herb Terry of Terry Lumber Company; Charlie Scofield, head carpenter; and many others—plasterers, painters, glaziers, landscape gardeners—were celebrating with us a job well done. Masses of white lilies, pink carnations, wine chrysanthemums surrounded the glistening white-and-mahogany pulpit, lectern, baptismal font.

Above the flowers against the reredos, white candles in shining brass holders and other brass furnishings cast a soft glow on the cross. All except the cross were memorials.

"The cross," Rev had explained, "can never be given as a memorial, because Jesus lives. Perhaps the children would like to give it." So Sunday School Superintendent Frank Berry had dropped to his knees to pray, as he always did, and prayed for that. The children had responded. John himself had preached a dozen sermons from the blue chair and brought his 'off'ring.' The gleaming cross there on the altar was the gift of the children of Bethel.

One child had been disappointed an hour before service, though, when I'd introduced him to Bishop McConnell. John had looked at me in surprise. No wings? No halo? "Mommy, is a Bishop only a man?"

Then a hush settled over the listening people, and even John by my side was unusually still. This Bishop, preaching, seemed a very special kind of man, making us all see clearly *'. . . the Lord, sitting upon a throne, high and lifted up . . . His train filling the temple.'*

"Dearly Beloved," intoned the dearly beloved old Bishop, *"it is meet and right that houses erected for the worship of God should be especially set apart and dedicated . . . to the cure of souls that doubt and to the persuasion of those that have not yet believed . . . to the relief of the distressed, the consecration of the strong, the guidance of the bewildered, the consolation of the dying . . .*

"We dedicate this church, made possible by your many sacrifices, in loving memory of all those whose hearts and hands have served . . .

"We dedicate this church with deep gratitude for loyal comrades who have made with us this spiritual adventure . . . deep gratitude for the unfailing courage, hard work, and determined faith of your young minister . . .

"We dedicate this church to the Glory of God, forever and ever. Amen."

I opened my purse for a pencil and scribbled the Bishop's words on the ***'Order for Dedication.' ". . . unfailing courage, hard work, determined faith of your young minister—"*** I wanted to remember what he'd said about my minister ***'forever and ever. Amen.'***

The episcopal dinner, course by course, came in the back door of the parsonage as I came in the front—fruit cocktail from Julie, hot yeast rolls from Minnie Stryker, Southern fried chicken from Mildred Piccarelli, cranberry jelly from Mother Thurner, and lemon meringue pie, four inches high, from Melissa and Edith. I thanked them, and put Julie's fruit cup on the table.

"Giving them all an opportunity to show love?" Rev teased, coming into the kitchen. We put our arms around each other. It had been a glorious morning.

"The best part," I whispered, "every word he said about you is true."

"Ha—you're prejudiced! Dinner ready? John's entertaining him—"

We walked into the living room. The Bishop was standing by the ninth window, his back toward us, bending down. John, reaching up, was holding the last blue drape, wrong side out, as close as he could get it to the Bishop's bifocals.

"See?" he was saying, as though it were something marvelous, like winning the Nobel Prize for Literature, "my mother sews with Scotch tape!"

"Humph!" Francis John cleared his throat, fingered the drape somewhat skeptically. "Let's hope she doesn't cook with it."

"Oh, no—she hardly cooks at all!" my little press agent went on. "The church ladies bring stuff in, and the neighbors—"

"Bishop," I said hastily, before my husband lost his new church, "won't you come in to dinner?"

"Bright boy you have here." The Bishop, peering from side to side and obviously wondering how much of everything was stuck together with tape, passed from the blue room through the pink room to the dining room. "Attractive parsonage, too—well kept-up."

"We fixed it all up for you," John got ahead of me. "It used to look like the dev—"

"Humph!" The Bishop cleared his throat again as he pulled out my chair. "Needn't have gone to any trouble for me. No need to fuss—"

"Sir," said my husband, "would you ask the blessing?"

I bowed my head, not listening to the Bishop's blessing . . . *'But I didn't, Bishop, go to any trouble for you . . . none at all . . . maybe I should have, but I didn't . . . it was all done, in love, for Marian Anderson, and for her, in love, I'd do it all again . . .'*

She has gone on, of course, to ever greater heights—first woman of her race to sing at the Metropolitan Opera House . . . winner of countless awards, degrees . . . delegate to the United Nations . . . known, loved, honored the world over—yet she is still Marian Anderson.

I remember the last time Rev and I heard her sing. We sat in the Bushnell Memorial in Hartford, with three thousand other hushed, silent people, listening to that great voice—***'the voice,'*** Toscanini had said, ***'that comes once in a century'***—and for the hundredth time I asked myself the secret of her greatness. Her voice, of course, but it was more than her voice. Then suddenly, in the hush, I knew the answer.

For this was the same hush that had fallen upon the people of Bethel the day the old Bishop blessed their church . . . the hush I had sometimes felt descend upon my husband's congregations as he pleaded for or prayed to his Lord . . . the hush that falls upon all people when they know they are truly loved. The secret is compassionate love.

Rev had sent a brief note backstage, the night of that last concert, telling Marian Anderson how much we had enjoyed it. The next morning there was a long-distance call. A soft voice asked, "May I speak to Mr. Grenfell? This is Marian Anderson." She had called to thank him for his note, for coming to hear her sing . . .

Love is the secret of Marian Anderson's greatness. Through her voice she pours out compassionate love upon us all, for like the old Bishop, like my husband, she, too, knows with tender sensitivity that each of us in today's mad world—no matter how successful, no matter how rich, no matter how brilliant—each of us without love is, in very truth,

". . . a motherless child,
A long way from home, a long way from home."

THE BEAUTIFUL METHODIST CHURCH on the main street of Bethel, Connecticut, scene of the Christmas Wedding.

. . . SEND THY BLESSING

O eternal God, creator and preserver of all mankind, giver of all spiritual grace, the author of everlasting life: Send thy blessing upon this man and this woman, whom we bless in thy name; that they may surely perform and keep the vow and covenant between them made, and may ever remain in perfect love and peace together, and live according to thy laws.

Look graciously upon them, that they may love, honor, and cherish each other, and so live together in faithfulness and patience. In wisdom and true godliness, that their home may be a haven of blessing and a place of peace; through Jesus Christ our Lord.

Amen.

". . . let the pealing organ blow
To the full-voiced choir below,
In service high and anthems clear
As may, with sweetness, through mine ear
Dissolve me into ecstasies,
And bring all heaven before mine eyes."

John Milton

CHRISTMAS, 1943

Shining and white in the heart of the town
Stands the church at Christmas time—
Its slender spires pointing upward to God,
Its doors open wide to men . . .

Through the open doors at Christmas time
The worshiping people come—
Mothers and sisters, sweethearts, dads,
Old men, and boys and girls—
The people come up the lighted walks
For the birthday of the Christ . . .
All the people come—except the young men.

Only the young men are not there,
The brave young men, the strong, the fair
Whom the church has reared and loved alway
On Christmas Day when the people pray
Are far and far away . . .

But not for a heartbeat does the church forget
And every bowing worshiper remembers yet
And every laughing boy and girl is in the debt
Of the young men far away . . .

Your church remembers when you, too, were boys—
Munching Christmas popcorn, eager for toys,
Sidling up to Santa when he called your name,
Sacrificing pennies when the offering came . . .

Your church remembers as you taller grew
Shepherds in costumes no shepherd ever knew,
Trailing weird draperies as wisemen from afar,
Atop the highest ladder to hang the Christmas star,
Dragging in the evergreens, fingers red with cold,
Then trooping off acaroling to the sick and old . . .

Your church remembers as the candles gleam red
That, kneeling, you took the Wine and the Bread
And Christ for your Captain on the road ahead—
The Christ who teaches that death is a door
Through which we pass to life evermore.

Now as the Christmas bells gladden the air,
Heads are lifted that were bowed in prayer
To the stars on the service flag hanging there
In the church that remembers you . . .

Now as the Christmas bells peal out once more,
We long for happier Christmases that lie before
When you, too, will walk through the open doors
Of the church that remembers you . . .
The church that is waiting and praying for you.

THE CHRISTMAS GIFTS I REMEMBER BEST

from my Father . . .

Love of God: The Father, Son, and Holy Ghost
Love of the Druid Mystery shot through all creation
Love of ministered to and ministering
Love of the laughter that harms not and eases much
Love of what hands can do with wood and stone
Love of worship and prayer and Holy Writ
Love of wife: how to husband through good and ill
Love of children: how to be a father to them
Love of unspoken things, well understood
Love of times past, a goodly heritage

from my Mother . . .

Love of Truth, and the adventure of seeking it
Love of the natural world's uplifting beauty
Love of language, respected and properly employed
Love of poetry and things whereof it speaks
Love of all kinds of singing and music
Love of industry and satisfaction in achievement
Love of learning and teaching
Love of woods and waters and wonders in Maine
Love of womankind, profoundly free
Love of times future and the promise of the new

John Millard Grenfell
December 25, 1973

A VERY SPECIAL CHRISTMAS PRESENT

"Did you get it yet?" Billy Fancher asked for the tenth time. Behind Billy, the tallest, were six other impatient choristers—all wearing high Eton collars, flowing black bow ties, and too-small white surplices, stained now with drops of red wedding punch, crumbs of chocolate cake.

"No—not yet. Be patient, boys." But patience was wearing thin. They'd waited now for nearly two hours—ever since Rev's ***'I now pronounce you man and wife'*** in the sanctuary upstairs. Waited through the long receiving line, the picture-taking, the cutting of the wedding cake. Waited for the best man to give Rev the little envelope so that Rev could give it to me so that I could give it to them. It was Christmas Eve. They wanted their two dollars each as promised, so they could run across the street to English Drug Store, buy the perfume, powder, scented soap or whatever they'd picked out for their mother's present and run home with it—fast.

"Can't Rev just ask him for it?" Burton, Billy's brother, wanted to know.

"No, he can't. Go eat some more cake, boys."

"Ladies said not to," Gardiner Warren answered. "Besides, it's hard to swallow. These collars are killing us. Can't we take this stuff off?"

"No," I said again, remembering what was under the once-white surplices—red flannel shirts, blue dungars—garb not quite suitable for a formal wedding reception. Rev was looking at me again, and so were several others, surrounded as I'd been for the past two hours by white surplices. I knew what Rev was thinking: *Looks exhausted. Why doesn't she go home?* I knew what the others were thinking, too: *Looks as if she might deliver any minute. Why doesn't she go home?*

"Be patient, boys," I said again. "It can't be much longer."

"Better not be," Billy said ominously. "Store closes at eight. Half-past seven right now."

"Don't worry—go sit for awhile." They unglued themselves, reluctantly.

I couldn't be hard on them. They'd sung like angels. Their ***Good Christian Men, Rejoice! Rejoice!***—the ***JOY! JOY!*** and the ***PEACE! PEACE!*** shouted at the top of their voices—had thrilled everyone, and there'd been hardly a dry eye during their tender, plaintive ***Silent Night***—the two carols Ed Bassett had especially asked for when he'd written Rev from Guadalcanal. He was coming home on two weeks' leave, he'd said, to marry Frannie Finger on Christmas Eve. Would Mrs. G. have her Boys' Choir sing those carols . . . How was she, by the way?

How she was, by the way, was eight months' pregnant, but thrilled, nonetheless, by the thought of a Christmas Eve wedding in the new sanctuary. Thrilled, too, by the thought of the little envelope. She wanted to give Rev a very special present this year—he'd worked hard, not only on the church, but on the parsonage, too. She'd noticed a set of matched, silver hair brushes in English Drug. Ten dollars . . . maybe, just maybe . . .

Everyone else in the parish had been thrilled, too. They'd all been sorry, reading about Marian Anderson, that Rev hadn't been able to marry the famous singer in their church . . . all been wondering who would have the first wedding there. No other couple could have pleased them more. Frannie Finger, Yorke's girl—blonde, beautiful, gentle—had been known and loved since birth. As for Ed Bassett, didn't know him so well, but he was a serviceman, wasn't he, been over there two years, and Frannie loved him . . .

So everyone had set to work—headed for the woods to pick hemlock tips, bent coat hangers from triangles to circles, tied them with fragrant green, trimmed them with long red-velvet bows, climbed ladders, hung wreaths in every window. Then they'd started fussing over the food. On Guadalcanal, Frannie said, servicemen had lived for six months on nothing but Spam.

The new sanctuary had, indeed, been beautiful that Christmas Eve, and the refreshment tables in the hall below laden with platter after platter of dainty hors d'oeuvres—lobster, shrimp, turkey, crabmeat. But dainty hors d'oeuvres disappear fast under the onslaught—and continued stay—of seven teenage boys. An hour into the reception Maude Hawley and Rita Anderson had made a mad dash for the First National, come back with long loaves of bread, peanut butter, grape jelly.

"Caverns they've got!" Maude had hissed in my ear in passing. "Not stomachs!"

Yes, I was the one responsible for the Boys' Choir—had organized it, robed it, directed it—and when Ed had last heard them sing in December, 1941, they'd been an active, fun-loving group of junior high youngsters. But much can happen to junior high youngsters in two years. They start playing football and dating girls and don't care much about wearing long black skirts. Things happen to voices, too. Sopranos quiver, tremble, slide down to baritones. Altos turn into basses.

Things also happen to the director and her family. The baby, sleeping or cooing during rehearsals in the carriage beside the piano, turns into the inquisitive little boy racing around the church hall, picking up containers of the acid workmen use to melt tin roofs on steeples, burning the cloth of his new snowsuit right through to his bare belly button. "Swallowed any," the doctor'd said, "he'd be dead." The director had given up the Boys' Choir at that point. It hadn't met for months. But now—Ed Bassett wanted boys to sing at his wedding.

I'd sent a note to the Youth Fellowship. Would they like to meet in the parsonage Sunday night? toast marshmallows? sing a few carols?

They would. Marshmallows disappeared by the bagful. I'd gone to the piano after awhile, begun playing ***Good Christian Men.*** A few left the fireplace, gathered round.

"Boy," Billy said, "how we used to yell the ***NEWS! NEWS!*** and the ***JOY! JOY!***"

"Yea, and the ***PEACE! PEACE!***" Gardiner added. "We sure made the church ceiling quiver!"

"Try it again, boys." I'd played loud. The parsonage ceiling had also quivered. But when I'd told them Ed's request, things quieted down.

What motivation to use . . . Patriotic? Lieutenant Bassett was a soldier, in the Pacific for two whole years . . . Religious? what would a Christmas wedding be without carols? . . . Economic? I hadn't wanted to use that one, really wanted those silver brushes, but I'd had to—explain about wedding honorariums, little envelopes, offer to share . . .

"How much will it be?" Billy wanted specifics. Well, ten, maybe . . . if all seven sang, that would be a dollar-fifty each. They still looked doubtful. Perhaps fifteen, I'd said hopefully. That would be two dollars each.

"And one left over," Burton was good at math. Yes, one left over. Not enough for silver brushes. We'd finally made an agreement, shaken hands. Two dollars each for singing two carols. Any less in the little envelope I'd make up. Any more would be all mine.

So they'd sung—black skirts worn low on the hips, Eton collars made larger with linked safety pins concealed by flowing black bows, white surplices providentially cut full. Ed, handsome in his white uniform, and Frannie, starry-eyed, had thanked each one. Others, knowing nothing of our financial agreement, had been surprised and pleased.

Minnie Rinnie, organist: "Love to see young people taking an interest in sacred music!"

Fred Johnson, choir director: "How about coming around to Adult Choir, boys? Getting a little big for those outfits!"

And Rev, with an odd look at me, "Mighty nice of you boys to do this, especially on Christmas Eve. Aren't you anxious to be getting home?"

Only the ladies in charge of the food had not been too pleased as seven boys stayed on and on and on, ate on and on and on . . .

"Did you get it yet?" Billy again. "They're leavin'!" And they were . . . running out, we saw as the doors opened, into falling snow.

"Goodbye! Goodbye! . . . God bless!" Confetti, rice, an old shoe or two for luck mixed with the white flakes. They were gone. Bill Shaw took his broom from the closet, began sweeping confetti. Maude and Rita gathered empty platters, headed for the kitchen. Seven boys looked at me. What now? Suddenly the best man was back, passing Rev something. Rev had it a very short time. Outside, on the snowy sidewalk, encircled by outstretched hands, I opened the little envelope—a five and a five and a five. *Thank you, dear Ed!*

The boys ran across the street. I followed as fast as possible. Mr. English, turning off lights, turned them on again for new business, changed fives to ones. I settled my accounts, went past the silver brushes without looking, picked up a dollar bottle of ***Old Spice,*** and slowly, laboriously walked home.

Rev was in the kitchen making tea. "I—I suppose you're wondering why I was in such a rush—what I did with the envelope."

"Not at all, dear. It's always yours. Certainly don't have to tell me what you buy."

"Well, I'd rather not, if you don't mind. After all, it's Christmas."

"What I'm really wondering—" Rev set his white cup, my blue one on the tray—"is how the seven little angels are spending ***their*** share."

"Share!" I stormed. "They got almost all of it! Two dollars each I had to promise—and I wanted so much to give you something special this year—"

"You gave Ed something special, darlin', a memory to take back across the Pacif—Listen! . . . Do you hear something?" Rev went to the window, opened it.

"NEWS! NEWS!
Give ye heed to what we say!
Jesus Christ is born today!"

He beckoned for me to stand beside him, laid one hand on my shoulder, the other gently on the coming child. ***Even the unborn,*** we'd read, ***can hear music*** . . . .

Red flannel shirts, blue dungars rapidly turning white . . . not surplices, not angelic garb, but the same angelic voices . . . high and clear . . . blown into our open window on snowflakes . . . blown sweetly, joyfully into our home . . . into our hearts . . . into our child—

"Now ye hear of endless bliss!
Jesus Christ was born for this!
PEACE! PEACE! . . .
Calls you one and calls you all
To gain his everlasting hall!
Christ was born to save!
Christ was born to save!"

"Merry Christmas, Rev! ***PEACE! PEACE!*** Mrs. G!" Laughter, shouts, as they ran down the street . . . ***"NEWS! . . . JOY!"***

"Now that," said my minister, closing out the snowflakes, "is what I call a special Christmas present—"

He turned, looked at me—"And another very special Christmas present still to come . . . go up to bed, my love . . . I'll bring our tea."

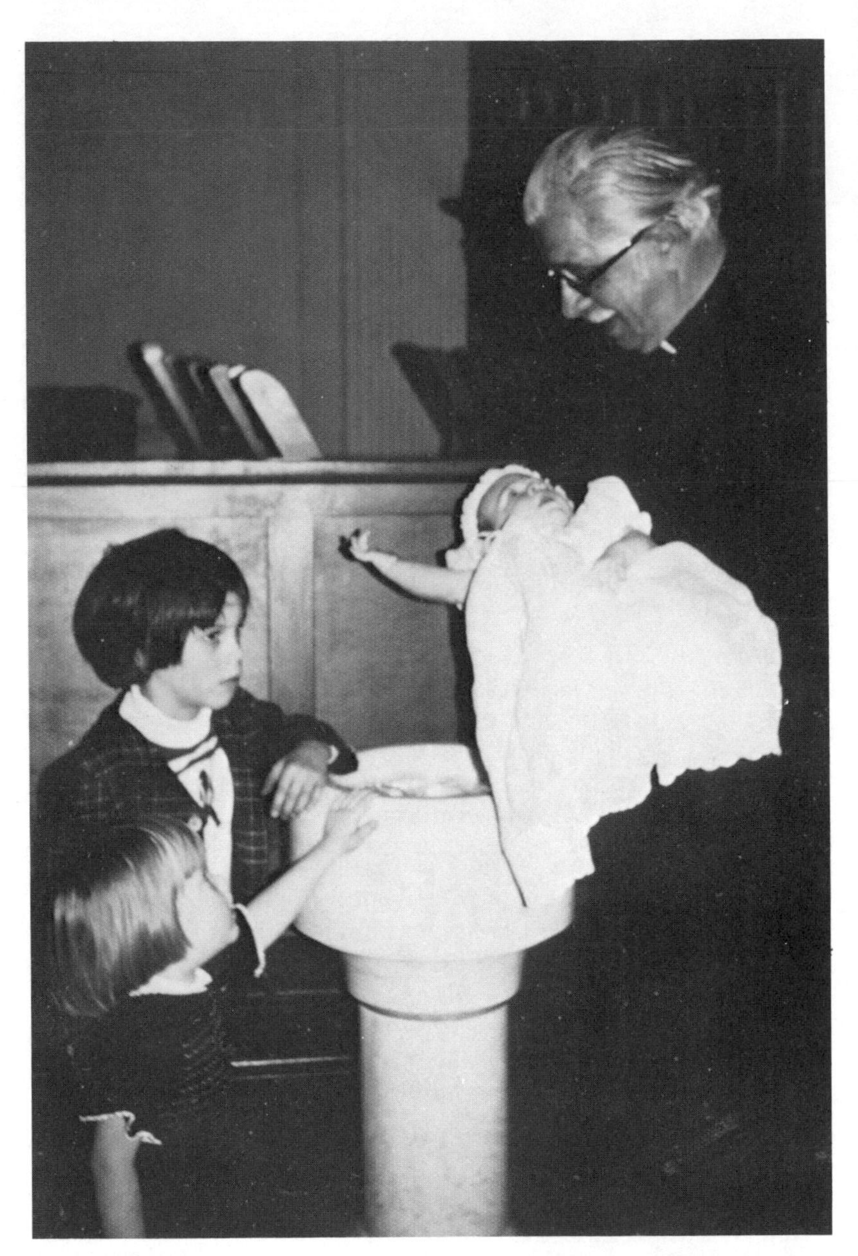

BAPTIZING SEVEN GRANDCHILDREN between 1968 and 1975 was ***'a part of ongoing creation'*** *that brought much joy. Here Jeb and Clara Bowron watch as Grandpa christens St. John Grenfell Bowron in Summerfield Methodist Church, Staten Island, New York, where his uncle and godfather, the Reverend John Grenfell, is pastor.*

. . . THE WORLD TO COME

Our Father, who art in heaven, hallowed be thy name. They kingdom come, thy will be done on earth as it is in heaven. Give us this day our daily bread. And forgive us our trespasses, as we forgive those who trespass against us. And lead us not into temptation, but deliver us from evil. For thine is the kingdom, and the power, and the glory, forever. Amen.

God, the Father, the Son, and the Holy Spirit, bless, preserve, and keep you; the Lord graciously with his favor look upon you, and so fill you with all spiritual benediction and love that you may so live together in this life that in the world to come you may have life everlasting.
Amen.

"Perhaps the best . . . of any and all true love . . . is the
resume . . . long
afterwards, looking at the actualities away back past, with
all their practical
excitations gone. How the soul loves to float amid such
reminiscences! So here
I sit gossiping in the early candlelight of old age—I and my
book—casting
backward glances over our traveled road."

Walt Whitman

ALWAYS

Always the thought of you, my love,
Always the thought of you—
Deep in my heart where I truly live
Always the thought of you . . .

Under the myriad words I say,
The myriad things I do,
Tender and warm in my hidden heart
Always the thought of you . . .

Always the memory of your face,
The eyes, the hands I knew—
Lighting my life from a secret place
Always the thought of you . . . .

CHARRED LOGS

"Are you happy, dear?" *he asks. She sits on the rug,*
Head against his knee . . . his fingers now and then
Touching her hair . . . The fire burns low—charred logs,
Too far apart, too separate . . . Soon, she knows,
He'll stand, take tongs in hand, lift gently till
The black sticks, side by side, blaze up again . . .

Could people do the same—old people, charred
With living, separate, alone? Could they
Ignite new fires for comfort? warmth? for light
On the darkening way?

To her left the ribboned bow,
The jeweler's box . . . to her right the tiny vase
Of woodland flowers he'd bent to pick—columbine,
The Star of Bethlehem—then given her
With a grin still boyish, young . . .
They'd shared a meal,
White candles gleaming soft on the crocheted cloth
Brought when he'd cleared away his mother's things.
He'd cooled champagne, proposed a toast: ***"To all***
The years behind and all the years ahead!"

"Are you happy, dear?", *he asks again. She turns,*
Looks up into his face—the same dear face
She'd known long years ago when all was young,
Wishes with all her heart she could answer, 'Yes!
Oh, yes, I'm happy—happy, dear!' . . . but no—

Happy's *a word for another, vanished day . . .*
Not in his power to give . . . or take away.

'. . . TILL DEATH DO US PART'

Into the emptiness between us now,
Into the void, immeasurable and wide,
I fling these words to ease the severed vow,
Knowing that words and words alone abide.

'A SACRED RITE . . .'

'Part of Creation—Ongoing Creation'

"Not a sacrament, of course," Rev had said to me, trying to explain why he could not marry people between beers at a tavern, "but a sacred rite . . . part of creation—ongoing creation. I have to give it His blessing."

He gave the blessing of the church—of Father, Son, and Holy Spirit—to literally hundreds of marriages. It was a function of his long ministry that he thoroughly enjoyed—all the way from talking things over beforehand (now, of course, it is termed 'pre-marital counseling'), to the wedding rehearsal, where his jokes and teasing put everyone at ease, to the sacred ceremony itself, and then to the fun, food, and fellowship of the reception.

He also enjoyed the 'ongoing' part of the marriages he performed—baptizing the children that came along, attending tenth, twenty-fifth, or even later anniversary parties . . . sometimes even marrying the offspring he'd baptized. Marriages that endured and prospered gave him joy. Those that didn't grieved him deeply. He willingly gave long hours of the more difficult 'post-marital counseling' to those who came back for help.

"Just the two of them?" I called, pulling into our drive as a young couple, the girl carrying a small bouquet, preceded Rev up the church steps. He turned back, license and ***Ritual*** in hand, came down the steps, leaned in the open car window.

"Just the two of them," he smiled as he kissed me, "and, of course, the Someone Else who is always there."

Somehow Rev always made those at his weddings—both participants and listeners—very much aware of the Someone Else who is always there. It was not unusual for a couple he'd never seen be-

Pamela Margaret
Mount Holyoke College, 1969

Miranda, 5 years

fore to come up to him, hand-in-hand, during the reception.

"We'd been talking divorce, Reverend, but somehow . . . after listening to that service today . . . well, anyway, we're going to give it another try."

"Stop by my office sometime soon . . . we'll talk things over."

Doctrinally liberal, non-conformist in many ways, Rev was highly traditional in his respect for and love of the rituals of the church. In his deep Cornish voice he intoned the beautiful words—***". . . in token and pledge of the vow between us made . . . and thereto I plight thee my troth . . ."*** never hurriedly, nor automatically but with the full force of his own belief. He believed in commitment. He believed in marriage.

Sometimes Rev would be asked to marry a couple who had written their own service. Sometimes he would be asked to combine two rituals—Catholic and Protestant, Christian and Jewish—but because he loved best the old words from the ***Book of Common Prayer***, that service is reprinted in this book. Perhaps some couple—too excited, too abstracted really to hear the words at their own wedding—will reread the centuries-old service, think about its meaning, and, if their marriage has in some way faltered, decide to renew their vows, to make a new commitment, 'give it another try.'

". . . part of creation—ongoing creation," Rev had said. The 'ongoing part' of his own marriage that brought him the greatest joy was, of course, our three children. Rather than a generation gap, they and their father had been closest during the ***Sixties*** when all three were undergraduates—John at Drew, the girls at Mount Holyoke. He had agonized with them over the bombing in Birmingham, the murders at Kent State, the Vietnam War. Each has willingly contributed to this book of their father's early marriages.

The opening poem is by Pamela, written when she was fifteen, a student at Darien High. Her sheaf of verse, sent annually at Christmas, was always her father's favorite gift—opened last, because the best, read sometimes with smiles, sometimes tears, but always with amazed delight at the perceptive insight and sensitivity of this loved younger daughter.

Lornagrace—born shortly after the events of the Christmas wedding narrated herein, always called ***Lady Dugal*** by her adoring father—has taken time from her crowded life as career woman and mother of three to give generous advice on photography and art. It was Lorna's suggestion that the cross and chi rho entwined by two

Lornagrace
Mount Holyoke College, 1966

Jeb, 11 years

Clara, 9 years

St. John, 7 years

rings—often called the Wedding Ring Cross and often used by her father—be used as a symbol to embellish the book.

Those who marry often become parents and then grandparents. Years before a special Grandparents' Day was instituted, the Reverend Dr. John annually honored such in his churches. Often he would invite his father to come preach the sermon. The book closes with John's ***Prayer of Many Years***, written for such occasions.

In each of the nine places we lived, Rev always found a coffee shop, a small restaurant, a 'hole in the wall' where he went for mid-morning coffee—the ***Sugar Bowl*** in Darien, Joe and Annie Klein's ***Sandwich Shop*** in Hartford, ***Willie's*** in Woodbury. "He'd wander in," Charlotte Banks of ***Sam's*** in Bethel wrote me thirty years after we'd left there, "have his coffee, talk. Everyone would gather round his booth. He made our day."

During the seven years of his retirement in West Hartford, the chosen coffee shop was ***Friendly's***, off Mountain Road. Here Rev went daily to chat with Ed Doran, the florist, other town merchants, a professor or two from Trinity, and, of course, the staff. We went to ***Friendly's*** for a last cup of coffee after the closing, the day we sold our Connecticut home to move to Maine.

"This is Susan Simmons," I said to the waitress, standing pad in hand. "She just bought our house. She'll be coming in here," I added jokingly, "to take Rev's place."

The waitress—plain, middle-aged, straight hair drawn back in a bun—did not smile. "No one," she said flatly, "can take Reverend Jack's place."

And, for many of us, no one can. Funny, kindly, humble, a completely non-threatening, completely approachable, completely honest and unpretentious man, Jack Grenfell was everybody's minister. There is in this book only one famous person, and her wedding was perhaps the least pretentious of all—but it has endured for more than forty years, as did Rev's.

Brides—hurrying from their reception, flushed, happy, sprinkled with confetti—would sometimes turn back, give me another hug, whisper, "Only hope our marriage will be as good as yours and Rev's!"

I could make no better wish for those who read this book—

And I would add one other: that the Someone Else who is always there be present in their lives—***". . . for better, for worse, for richer, for poorer, in sickness and in health . . ."***—as He was, and is, present in the life of my husband and the woman he married.

John Millard
Drew University, 1963

Tamarleigh, 8 years

Trelawney, 6 years

Tallessyn, 6 years

PRAYER OF MANY YEARS

(To be said by all Grandparents present)

Heavenly Father,
May the years of our age be the sweetest of all.
May we neither leave our dreams behind,
Nor let our hopes grow cool,
Nor fear to look ahead,
Nor let the fires of the spirit die,
Nor the winter of the body chill the eternal springtime of the heart.

Help us to love and cherish the very best from life—
No matter that the years fly,
No matter that much of the world we knew has now gone by.

And may 'old age' always be just a few years older than we. ***Amen.***

John Millard Grenfell
Summerfield United Methodist Church
Staten Island, New York

"She reads flawlessly!"

Robert Kyff, teacher
Kingswood-Oxford School, West Hartford, CT

"A fantastic speaker for any major occasion!"

Dr. Elbert Cole, Pastor
Central United Methodist Church, Kansas City, MO

"Presence, dignity, poise, a strong voice under fine control—she might have been an actress, a Helen Hayes sort of actress, bringing life to words."

Dr. Winthrop C. Libby, President Emeritus
University of Maine, Orono, ME

"She made me cry."

Suzanne Fox, Class of '87
Bowdoin College, Brunswick, ME

* * * * *

Clarine Coffin Grenfell is a native of Bangor, Maine, but has spent much of her adult life as educator and writer in New York and Connecticut. She earned her Bachelor of Arts at University of Maine with Phi Beta Kappa honors and her Bachelor of Divinity at Hartford Theological Seminary. She has been at various times the pastor of Methodist churches, chairperson of Departments of English, editor and reading consultant in the Educational Division of *Reader's Digest*. Previous publications include textbooks, religious drama, verse, and non-fiction. Married for many years to the late Reverend Jack Grenfell, Mrs. Grenfell is the mother of a son and two daughters. She is presently director of the Grenfell Reading Center in Orland, Maine. A popular speaker throughout her career, she especially enjoys sharing her prose and verse with live audiences.

* * * * *

Since the publication in 1982 of her first book of reminiscences—***The Caress and the Hurt,*** now in its fifth printing—Clarine Coffin Grenfell has shared her *'Prose and Verse'* with live audiences totaling more than thirty thousand people of all ages and, through radio and television, with many more. It is a form of ministry she much enjoys. No honorarium or fee is involved. If you would like to order books or invite her to speak at your school, church, club, or library, you may write directly to Grenfell Reading Center, Orland, ME 04472.